Writing Skills
For Parents

WRITING SKILLS FOR PARENTS

Irene Yates

Piccadilly Press • London

Text copyright © Irene Yates, 1996

All rights reserved. No part of this publication may be
reproduced, stored in a retrieval system, or transmitted in any
form or by any means electronic, mechanical, photocopying,
recording or otherwise, without the prior permission of the
copyright owner.

The right of Irene Yates to be identified as Author of this work has
been asserted by her in accordance with the Copyright, Designs
and Patents Act 1988.

Phototypeset from author's disk by Piccadilly Press.
Printed and bound by WBC, Bridgend
for the publishers Piccadilly Press Ltd.,
5 Castle Road, London NW1 8PR.

A catalogue record for this book is available from the British
Library

ISBN: 1 85340 410 1

Irene Yates lives in Redditch, Worcs. She was a primary school
teacher specialising in literacy skills for 16 years. She is now an
educational writer and consultant.

Material from the National Curriculum is Crown Copyright and is reproduced by permission of the Controller of HMSO.

BARNSLEY LIBRARIES	
38059400014355	
J M L S	**15/01/97**
GO	**£5.99**
371.302813	

Contents

Introduction

What Is Writing? xiii
Is Writing Squiggles (The Medium),
   Or What It's Saying (The Message)?

Why Children Might Dislike Writing xiv
Difficulty
Fear Of Criticism

How Can You Help Your Child To Like Writing? xv

You Can Make A Difference xvi

1. What Is Writing All About?

How Do You View Writing? 1

How Your Child Sees Writing 1

What The Teacher Is Looking For 2

The Dynamics Your Child Faces 3

Finding Out Your Child's Ideas About Writing 4

**The Importance Of Helping Your Child
   Understand The Magic Of Writing** 6
Practical Activities 7

2. WHAT THE CHILD WRITES AND THE ACT OF WRITING IT

PRODUCT AND PROCESS   9
Which Is Most Important?

WHAT DOES YOUR CHILD THINK WHEN WRITING?   10

ON ONE SIDE THE CREATOR, ON THE OTHER SIDE THE CRITIC   11

WRITING AS A LANGUAGE SKILL   11
Listening And Speaking
Reading And Writing
Interaction Of Language Skills

PRACTICAL ACTIVITIES   14

3. AT WHAT STAGE OF WRITING IS YOUR CHILD?

STAGES IN WRITING   17
First Stage: Scribble Writers
Second Stage: Experimental Writers
Third Stage: Early Writers
Fourth Stage: Writers Using Some Of The Conventions
Fifth Stage: Proficient Writers

EVALUATING YOUR CHILD'S WRITING   19
The Problems Of Only Looking At The End Result
How The Teacher's Constraints Affect Work

HOW DO CHILDREN IMPROVE THEIR WRITING?	23

AN EXPERIMENT TO HELP YOU UNDERSTAND YOUR CHILD'S WRITING SKILLS	24

Understanding Your Child's Thought Processes
Evaluating The Two Pieces

PRACTICAL ACTIVITIES	27

Set Up A Writing Corner
Writing Tasks

4. THE DIFFICULTIES OF WRITING AND HOW YOU CAN HELP

WHAT MAKES WRITING SO HARD?	29

Writing Involves Many Skills
Thinking Of Something To Write About

HELPING YOUR CHILD TO BE POSITIVE TOWARDS WRITING	31

Writing For The Fun Of It
Don't Worry About The Mistakes
Everyday Events Are Brilliant Ideas To Write About
Be A 'Wider Audience' For Your Child

HELP YOUR CHILD DEAL WITH 'MARKING'	37

PRACTICAL ACTIVITIES	39

Surround Your Child With Literature
Shared Writing
Publishing Writing

5. LEARNING THE RULES OF WRITING

GRAMMAR 45
Why Grammar Is So Difficult to Learn
How Grammar Is Taught In Schools

PUNCTUATION 49
Full Stops
Question Marks
Speech Marks
Apostrophes
Commas
Helping Your Child With Punctuation

SPELLING 51
First Attempts At Spelling
Asking For Help
How Spelling Is Taught In Schools
Invented Spelling
How Children Themselves Learn To Spell
What Problems Do Children Have With Spelling?

HANDWRITING 56
The Stages of Developing Handwriting
How Handwriting Affects Composition Or Message

LOCATING PROBLEM AREAS 58
Getting Samples Of Writing To Compare

DEALING WITH YOUR CHILD'S WORRIES 59

CONFUSING NORMAL STAGES OF DEVELOPMENT WITH REAL PROBLEMS — 60

PRACTICAL ACTIVITIES — 61
Reinforcing Grammar
Reinforcing Punctuation
Reinforcing Spelling
Reinforcing Handwriting

6. WRITING IN SCHOOLS

DIFFERENT KINDS OF WRITING IN SCHOOLS — 71
Creative Writing
Factual Writing

METHODS OF TEACHING WRITING — 72
Whole Language Approach
The Traditional Approach

WRITING IN NURSERY/INFANT SCHOOL — 75

WRITING IN JUNIOR SCHOOL — 77

THE NATIONAL CURRICULUM — 78
What Children Are Taught In The National Curriculum
Drafting
SATS
Preparing Your Child For Tests

SCHOOL COMPUTERS AND WRITING	85
PRACTICAL ACTIVITIES	87
Drafting	
Discussing Work	

7. SUMMARY

KEEP YOUR CHILD MOTIVATED	92
The Need For A Reason To Write	
An Audience For Writing	
HOW WRITING AT HOME INSTILS CONFIDENCE	94
Children Feel Less Anxious At Home	
The Child Has A Choice Of Situations In Which To Work	
Children Are More Confident At Home	
Children Feel Less Pressurised At Home	
ABOVE ALL – BE ENTHUSIASTIC YOURSELF	97

APPENDICES

INTRODUCTION

Ask children what writing is, and they'll come up with varying answers, such as:

It's something you have to learn to do so your teacher can mark it.

It's something that will help you get a job if you do it properly.

It's about writing stories and poems and things.

It's something you learn. Some people are good at it.

It's something you have to keep tidy and try not to make mistakes.

It's a way of communicating things that are in your head when you don't want to talk about them.

WHAT IS WRITING?

IS WRITING SQUIGGLES (THE MEDIUM), OR WHAT IT'S SAYING (THE MESSAGE)?

You can see from the above replies that there's a great muddle in children's minds about whether writing is important for its own sake or for the sake of its conventions. In other words, which has priority – the *medium*, i.e. the squiggles on the page, or the *message*, i.e. what the writing is saying?

In a sense that muddle sums up all the problems of

writing. It shows that 'writing' has two strands to it.

The *medium* is anything to do with the presentation, including handwriting, spelling, grammar.

The *message* is anything to do with the idea that's being communicated, including choice of words and ideas.

Most children will tell you that they think writing is 'very important' but they won't be able to tell you why! It seems that once they start school they rapidly pick up the idea that everything they do will be assessed by means of their writing ability. This means not just their ability to communicate an idea or a thought, but their skills in writing legibly, spelling correctly, understanding grammar and punctuation.

WHY CHILDREN MIGHT DISLIKE WRITING

DIFFICULTY
Sometimes children say:
'I know what I want to say but I just can't seem to put it down on paper.'

Here, children want to make messages of one kind or another, and yet something stops them.

FEAR OF CRITICISM
It seems to me that the way we teach writing has an awful lot to do with their fear of criticism. When you ask children, *'What stops you?'* the replies are always: *'I can't spell,' 'I'm no good at grammar,' 'People will just laugh at it,' 'I haven't got the confidence,' 'I don't know where to put the commas,' 'Nobody can read my writing.'*

Those replies all add up to the same thing. Fear of criticism. They want to use this skill of writing but they're afraid that what they produce will not be acceptable for any one or more of those reasons. So they are reluctant to write.

How Can You Help Your Child To Like Writing?

REMEMBER, CHILDREN NEED TO LEARN THE PROCESS

The problem is, if you don't practise the skill you don't get any better at it. And if you don't make the mistakes you don't learn how to put them right! What you have to do is accept that writing is a *process* – something you learn over a long period of time. Expecting to be able to pick up a pencil and write in a conventional way without mistakes as soon as you know what a pencil is, is like expecting to be able to design and build a house when you only know what a brick is!

REMEMBER THEIR FIRST ENTHUSIASM

Children are natural born writers. From the moment they can hold a crayon in their hands they're desperate to make their squiggles on the page and proclaim their precious stories to you. At this point they haven't a clue whether there's anything 'wrong' with their writing or not. Their enthusiasm knows no bounds. So what happens to change it? What happens that turns happy little children from churning out story upon story into reluctant learners who'd do anything rather than put pen to paper?

YOU CAN MAKE A DIFFERENCE

This book sets out to show you how you can help your child. It will tell you how writing is taught in schools and why your children may find it hard. It will show you how to help them. It's not aimed at any particular age group: it's for anyone who can hold a writing tool, be they twelve months old or eighteen years. It gives practical advice and activities that you can develop with your children. It shows you how spelling, grammar and punctuation work and gives you ways of acquainting your children with the rules.

Above all, it will teach you how you can help your children to learn to write just for the joy of it. Because once they can do that they can write anything.

Chapter One

WHAT IS WRITING ALL ABOUT?

HOW DO YOU VIEW WRITING?

It might help to get your own mind clear at this point if you would ask yourself some questions:
What do I think writing is?
What importance do I attach to writing?
What do I write?
What do I think are the good features about my own writing and what do I think are the poor features?
What do I want for my children as far as writing is concerned?

It might also be of value for you to actually *write* your answers rather than merely think them. Often when we write things down we come to different conclusions and just by actually writing we learn what it is we *know*, or what it is we really *think*.

HOW YOUR CHILD SEES WRITING

The writing that you do probably has a very clear purpose or function. Maybe you write shopping lists, or letters to relatives, or fill in forms, or put daily details of your life into your diary.

Whatever your reasons for writing you will always know what those reasons are.

It's not quite so clear-cut to children in school. They realise that they are, nine times out of ten, writing for someone else – not themselves. That someone else is usually a teacher. And, to the child's mind, teachers always have hidden reasons for doing things. Often children believe that, although the teacher asks for a 'story' or a 'poem' or a piece of factual writing, she is not so much interested in the ideas of that writing (the message) as in how correct and neat it is (the medium). They believe that their teacher measures them by what they produce in writing. That writing has no importance or use other than to show the teacher how 'good' or 'bad' they are at it.

Therefore, most children, on most occasions, perform *as they think their teachers expect them to*.

If they are asked for a story they write the story they think the teacher wants. If they are asked for a poem they do likewise. If they are asked for factual writing they write to demonstrate what they think they are supposed to have learned.

WHAT THE TEACHER IS LOOKING FOR

It is true that teachers are always keen to instruct. They look for spelling mistakes, for poor handwriting, for bad grammar or punctuation. These are things they feel impelled to point out with a red pen – though whether the children ever take any notice is a moot point, and whether the red pen has any positive effect whatsoever is debatable. (We will be looking further into this matter in Chapter 3 and Chapter 4.)

On the other hand, they are also always looking out for a creative streak, something that lifts the child's writing out of the ordinary into the realm of 'good' or 'very good'. Of course, they have only arbitrary means of making this judgement – but when you are marking thirty-five books day in, day out, you can very easily see the average, the below-average and the above-average. The writing tends to speak for itself! Of course, you have only the writing within your own class to form your judgement from. Even so, 'good' or 'sparkling' writing always tends to stand out from the crowd.

In the main, teachers' understanding of the role as facilitator in writing is that they must instruct the children, always, to do better.

THE DYNAMICS YOUR CHILD FACES

Children tend to feel that once they have sacrificed words to paper those words are written in concrete and cannot be changed. Professional writers think nothing of writing a single sentence twenty or thirty or fifty times until they get it exactly how they want it.

Nobody would suggest for one minute that a child should write each sentence over and over again. But contrast this attitude to the one of the child sitting over a piece of geographical writing when the teacher has ended her instructions on the writing with, *'And don't forget your full stops and capital letters!'*

You can see from this that there are a whole lot of dynamics going on in a classroom even before your child begins to put pen to paper. Many of these dynamics are to do with what the children think the teacher's expectations are!

Their starting point is, *'What does the teacher want?'* and the last instructions will usually stay uppermost in their minds.

This will influence their writing, and make an impact on the work they produce. That work will then be marked and judged – but from what angle?

FINDING OUT YOUR CHILD'S IDEAS ABOUT WRITING

Probably the most important thing you can do is find out what your children's ideas about writing are.

Ask the following questions, and try to get them to write down their answers. Assure them, if they're worried about whether they get the answers 'right' or 'wrong', that you're not interested in right or wrong, the spelling, the punctuation, the handwriting – you merely want to know what they think. Tell them there are no *right* or *wrong* answers – the answers are purely what they *believe*.

What Is Writing All About?

* Who are writers?
* What do writers do?
* What kind of things do they write?
* What happens to writing when it's written?
* Are you ever a writer?
* When do you write?
* Why do you write?
* What happens to your writing?
* What would you like to happen to your writing?
* What do you enjoy about writing?
* What do you not like about writing?
* What would you like to write most?

From the answers you should be able to form a pretty good interpretation of your child's attitudes towards writing and some understanding of how they see it. Use this knowledge to talk about writing with them. Don't force the issue, but let them tell you honestly and confidently what they feel about the activity. There will probably be areas where they feel they lack ability – say, *'Maybe we could work on this together and make some progress,'* or, *'I've been reading about this. I think I've got some ideas that might help.'*

The one thing that will not help them is to attach blame for any shortcomings. Bear in mind, at all times, that writing is a *process*, and that all processes have to be developed.

The Importance Of Helping Your Child Understand The Magic Of Writing

When children first begin to write they do so with no inhibitions or anxieties whatsoever. Their scribble stories are purely about *message*, about describing something that fills them with joy and makes them want to communicate with others.

Their knowledge is only that writing is a set of signs and symbols or scribbles on a page, and that each sign, symbol or scribble means something. This is when they are able to say to you, without any obstacle whatsoever, *'Look at my story. Let me read it to you!'* They are able, always, to tell you exactly what their scribbles mean.

The first thing most children learn to write *properly* is their name. They then take the almost tortuous step from complete freedom to total restraint (*. . .this is how you make a T for Tom; start at the top and come down, etc. . .*) and suddenly they understand that writing is a much harder thing than they ever thought it was. Now they realise that although *they* may understand their own scribbles, other people cannot – unless the scribbles are formed in special ways which make them recognisable to the reader.

Sometimes a really silly problem arises. They write their story and know exactly what they mean it to say. But because they have worked so hard to make their scribble distinguishable to the reader, to make it *correct*, they can no longer 'read' it themselves. This is because, in forming the 'right' shapes and letters for others, they have quite lost the meaning for themselves! This is when they come to you and say, *'What does it say? What have I written?'* as though the writing is out of their hands after all and is some kind of act of magic that they are not yet privy to.

The 'magic' is the *process of writing* and it is something they will be learning, practising and refining for all their schooldays and maybe far beyond.

PRACTICAL ACTIVITIES

* Try to remember that a writing child is a reading child. The two activities are always connected – if a child is writing then a child is reading.

* Give your children the opportunity to enjoy scribbling with crayons and pencils as soon as they can hold them in their hand. Let them have huge sheets of paper – the back of wallpaper is excellent – and scribble to their heart's content.

* Give them letters to trace. Use a highlighter pen and get them to go over the letter in a darker colour crayon or felt tip.

* Get them to practise drawing the shape of the letters in the air with their fingers. This will help them to get the 'feel' for the way the letter needs to be formed.

* Draw dotted letters and get them to join up the dots.

* The next step after tracing is copying. Print the letters very carefully, in lower case not capitals, making the sound of the letter at the same time. Let them copy the letters, starting at the right place. Give lots of encouragement and praise.

* Check the children are holding the writing tool correctly right from the beginning. It's easy to get into bad habits by starting with the wrong grip. The tool should be held lightly between the thumb and first finger, about 2 cm from the point. It takes lots of practice to develop control of the pencil. All drawing, tracing, copying or making pattern activities will help to develop what is called 'fine motor' control – i.e. using the fine muscles of the fingers and hands.

* If your children look as if they are going to be left handed, help them to develop their skills. It's not easy to write with the left hand because it involves pushing rather than pulling the pencil on the paper. Move the paper so that it is at an angle to the writer to make it easier. On no account try to force the writer to use the right hand – children need to be allowed to use which ever hand is dominant for them, otherwise confusion will result.

* Don't worry if they do mirror writing at times – writing letters and numbers backwards. This happens particularly with the 'b' and the 'd', and with numbers 2, 3, 5 and 7. Point out the mistake and suggest correcting it without making a fuss. This problem usually sorts itself out by the time the child is about seven.

Chapter Two

WHAT THE CHILD WRITES AND THE ACT OF WRITING IT

PRODUCT AND PROCESS

It is important to understand the difference between the *product*, i.e. what the child writes, and the *process*, the act of writing it.

The product is what we can look at, read, mark and correct. It's committed to paper, it shows us, perhaps, what the child can *do*.

The process is the act of putting together two strands – the strand of making up, composing, creating and the strand of getting the spelling right, learning about grammar and punctuation, refining handwriting skills.

WHICH IS MOST IMPORTANT?

If you can understand that products are mostly jumping-off points from which the writer moves to the next attempt at a product, then you can readily see that 'process' has to be the most important aspect to the development of writing skills.

The difficulty arises because the children have to focus on the product in order to go through the process

– so, in a way, you have to lead them to believe that each product, each piece of writing, is of great value in its own right. Otherwise they wouldn't be motivated to do it.

Of course their writing *is* valuable and you must always let them know that it is. If they get, for one moment, the idea that it hasn't any worth, other than 'keeping them occupied' they are halfway down the path to losing all motivation and then putting the brake on their skills' development.

Somehow between the process and the product you have to find just the right balance. Once you get into the routine of writing – hopefully for fun – with your children, then that balance will most likely find YOU.

WHAT DOES YOUR CHILD THINK WHEN WRITING?

Consider how many things a child is thinking about when trying to master the process.

First, there is the content: *What is the story going to say? What is its shape, its form? Who am I writing it for? What does that person expect of me? How long should it be?* Second, there are the conventions: *Is my handwriting okay? Should I slow down a bit, or write a bit faster? Should I have used a pencil instead of a pen? Have I spelt that word right? How do you spell xyz? Should I use a different word that I can spell? Have I remembered all the full stops? Where do the capital letters go? Did I do my margin the right size?* And so on, and so on.

There's a struggle going on constantly in the child's head. You can see that *thinking* is most definitely a part of the process – not just simple thinking either, but almost *multiple-process* thinking because there are so many thoughts to dwell on at once!

ON ONE SIDE THE CREATOR, ON THE OTHER SIDE THE CRITIC

Professional writers often think of themselves as the *'creator'* and the *'critic'*. The one dwells upon composition or content, the other dwells upon the technicalities. The interesting thing about it is that the first is a right-brained activity, and the second is a left-brained activity. The first uses imagination, the second uses analysis. It is quite possible for a writer to allow these two thinking activities to take place together, but more usual for a *professional writer* to allow the right-brained creative activity to have its say without inhibition first and then go back through the work with the left-brain switched on to work on the conventions.

Children, or beginning writers, are expected to have both thinking activities always working at the same time.

WRITING AS A LANGUAGE SKILL

Writing is arguably the hardest of the four major language skills. Those skills, which are constantly

developing throughout the whole of our lives, are:
Listening (Receptive)
Speaking (Active)
Reading (Receptive)
Writing (Active)

LISTENING AND SPEAKING

Education refers to *listening* rather than to *hearing* because in listening the brain is actively engaged in understanding and interpreting sounds. From listening, we learn to speak.

As a parent you will know from experience that once children begin to talk they experiment. They explore new words, new ways of putting them together, try out different ways of talking. The worst thing you can do is try to stop them, because once you discourage them from their exploration they will be afraid to talk in case they get things *wrong*.

From listening and speaking we begin to cultivate our thinking skills. And, as we have already seen, thinking is a large part of the writing process.

READING AND WRITING

Children who become interested in reading early increase their language skills at a much faster rate than those who never see a book.

This is not to say that children have to be *reading for themselves* but that the parents or carers who share books, stories, poems, nursery rhymes etc are actually building solid foundations for a child's reading and writing skills.

It's a print-rich world that we live in today and,

right from the beginning, children see and learn to recognise all kinds of writing. They see: cards, signs, newspapers, magazines, catalogues, slogans on T-shirts, billboards. They begin to understand the connection between print and communication and feel the urge to commit their own ideas and messages to paper.

INTERACTION OF LANGUAGE SKILLS

You cannot take the four language skills separately – they interact constantly and depend upon each other for development.

It is almost assumed that children learn to speak at home, and learn to read and write at school. But why should this be so? This view presupposes that all the writing that children see happen around them before they begin school is to be ignored. It also means that the new-to-school infant may think (and then *always* believe) that the reading and writing that happens in school is something different from that which happens at home or in the community.

It's much better to let the children experiment with reading and writing just as they experimented with talking. This way they begin to develop confidence and enjoyment in the activity – both of which are crucial to their later ability.

The basis of good writing is good thinking and planning, and/or good discussion.

PRACTICAL ACTIVITIES

* Right from babyhood you can talk to your children, take them to places, show them things and share experiences with them. Give them lots of encouragement to express all their ideas, thoughts and feelings, in speech and in scribble and pictures. Give them plenty of opportunities to develop their thinking skills, let them try and work things out for themselves. Encourage them to plan and negotiate ideas.

* Ask them questions that don't necessarily have a *'Yes'* or *'No'* answer. Ask them *'Why?'* and *'How?'* and *'What if?'*, even if you think they won't be able to formulate an answer. Often they'll surprise you! Don't make the mistake of knocking them down if they get answers wildly off-beam. Say, *'That's an interesting idea, I'm not sure it's right though. . .'* and go on to explain. At all times encourage them to develop their thinking skills so that when it comes to composing and creating they are happy to take their ideas and extend them, not think, *'Oh, I can't write that, everybody will say it's silly!'* Remember that later, when they begin creative writing, the imagination needs to take wing and not be scared of going in the 'wrong' direction!

* Have lots of coloured paper, pens, pencils and crayons in the house. Right from the moment they can hold a writing tool you can get them to write and draw their experiences. You can give the writing purpose by saying, *'Let's send Grandma a message,'* or, *'Let's write Lucy a birthday card,'* etc. etc. They can write messages for

WHAT THE CHILD WRITES AND THE ACT OF WRITING IT

Mum, Dad or the carer to read with them. They can write 'shopping lists' with their own needs on them to add to your own. Encourage them to tell you what their messages say, to support the link between reading and writing.

* When they write give them the courage and confidence to read back to you what they have written. If they're at the stage of judging their own work get them to turn off the *inner critic* until the creator is satisfied with the *message*. Then teach them how to proofread.

* With very young children you can make an alphabet wall chart together. You can use separate sheets of paper stuck together or one long sheet of wallpaper. Talk them through it as you're going along, e.g. *'Tell me something that begins with the sound "a"? That's right, an apple. Can you draw an apple for the chart? This is how you write "a".'* Don't try to do this activity all in one go, make it last a couple of weeks. Go back to the beginning and see what they can remember. This activity will help forge the links for letter recognition and identification.

* Use pictures as story-starts. Ask them to look at a picture hard and think about what's going on in it. Or what happened before the picture? What will happen after the picture? Catalogues are good for this kind of exercise. If they want to 'write' the story, cut the picture out and stick it on a sheet of paper which they can scribble their 'words' on. Get them to tell the story back to you. This activity will help to develop imagination.

* Use the back of large sheets of wallpaper and thick crayons to practise making signs and symbols on paper. Let your children write or scribble as 'big' as they can. Get them to practise making flowing lines and circles, and as many kinds of patterns as they can. Encourage complete freedom of movement. To help with later handwriting skills they need to develop good wrist manipulation as well as the ability to control the writing tool with their fingers.

* Encourage them to 'write' their own versions of stories that you've shared together or experiences that they have had. Don't worry, at this stage, about them trying to form the letters correctly – just encourage the free and confident making of marks upon the page. Always get them to 'read their story back to you' if they can, and help them if they have 'forgotten' what it says.

Chapter Three

AT WHAT STAGE OF WRITING IS YOUR CHILD?

STAGES IN WRITING

There are certain stages in the development of writing which, with a little practice, you will be able to identify quite easily. Any writer can be at any of these stages of writing development at any age though the average child (if such a body exists!) will most likely be at the first stage when beginning school and at the fourth or fifth stage when leaving. A mixed ability classroom will more than likely have children of the same age at all different stages so it is not always advisable to compare your child's work with that of others in the same class.

These are the basic stages though they are not exact or accurate and often they overlap. Sometimes a child may leap from one stage to another with hardly any time in between.

FIRST STAGE: SCRIBBLE WRITERS
At this stage, the writing just looks like scribble, it has no meaning for anyone other than the writer. But to be at this stage the writer has taken quite a bit of under-

standing on board. They understand that written symbols mean messages. They allocate a message to their scribble. They understand that reading and drawing are different.

Sometimes, you may be able to decipher certain letters. Scribble writers may be able to write or copy their name.

SECOND STAGE: EXPERIMENTAL WRITERS

At this stage the writing looks something like real writing, though it still may not make a lot of sense. But it shows that the writers understand that speech can be written down. They know that the message remains the same once it is written in symbols. They understand that the writing goes from left to right and down the page. They experiment with writing letters and words. At this stage, when they read their message back to you, you may be able to work out what some words are. For example 'saw' might be written as 'su' or 'my' might be written as 'mI'.

THIRD STAGE: EARLY WRITERS

At this stage, the message is very important. Writers choose things to write about which are significant to them. They understand the idea of 'audience' or 'reader'. They have the sense of sentence though they may not be able to cope with more than one element of writing at the same time. For example, if they are concentrating on spelling they may not be able to think about handwriting and punctuation. They experiment with writing words and language they are familiar with from reading and from the language around them.

They are conscious that spelling has to be correct and may attempt to spell new words from 'sounding out', or may be too frightened to attempt new words at all.

FOURTH STAGE: WRITERS USING SOME OF THE CONVENTIONS

Children are by now very familiar with the writing process and are aware of punctuation, spelling, grammar. They are able to plan and devise different ways of writing for different purposes. They can proof-read and edit their own work and may be anxious to have the opportunity to redraft so that they can make their own corrections before anyone looks at the work.

FIFTH STAGE: PROFICIENT WRITERS

Children have developed their own writing style and have control over spelling, punctuation and handwriting. They know what meaning they wish to convey with their message and have developed ideas so that they can express their creativity. They can organise their work in paragraphs, take notes and plan texts.

EVALUATING YOUR CHILD'S WRITING

To work out at what stage of writing your child is, you need to be able to look at their writing from two angles:

* evaluating the product – what they have actually written when their piece of work is finished or when they think it is finished.

* evaluating the *process* – that is, what was happening in their minds while they were in the act of writing it.

On the whole, we tend to focus mainly on product, that is, what the children have actually written. It is almost as if that product is absolute proof of their ability, as though the written work itself is the ultimate judge of competence.

In fact, the product tells you only half of it. You can often learn more from trying to find out exactly what's in the children's minds when they are actually doing the writing – that is, the thinking processes they are using.

THE PROBLEMS OF ONLY LOOKING AT THE END RESULT

A piece of writing can only tell you what went wrong or right at the exact time it was being written. But if the writer goes on to do a second, or third, draft of the piece of work you might find a completely different product.

When children are doing a first draft of, let's say, a story, it's quite possible that they are concentrating particularly on making that story exciting, giving it a beginning, middle and end, making it *work*. Because their brains are so focused on one particular aspect of producing the story they may make mistakes that they wouldn't normally make – such as in spelling, grammar, or handwriting. These mistakes may not occur if they were thinking about those particular skills. To illustrate this – children can often get all the spellings right in a test but get the same words wrong when they're using them in a piece of written work.

Given the chance to go on to do a second draft, often they will discover some of their 'silly' spelling or grammatical errors and put them right.

Frequently there isn't time to do the work again (redrafting) and judgement is made of their first effort, warts and all, so that, instead of being praised for what they have managed to do, they are reproached for the mistakes they've made.

It's always possible that, given the opportunity, in redrafting they can not only put their mistakes right, but also find ways of making the product even more interesting, by using different words to add more excitement, pace or flavour.

Because of the limits of time, more often than not, in school at least, the products of first drafts are taken away to be marked and assessed as though the quickly finished pieces of work are set in concrete.

HOW THE TEACHER'S CONSTRAINTS AFFECT THE WORK

This idea of words set in concrete is one that children in school are very familiar with.

Often they are given fairly tight constraints to work within. For example, their teacher will say, *'We have to get this writing finished before playtime.' 'Write me a poem about what you did on Saturday.' 'Write me a story about your birthday party.'*

Most of the time it doesn't occur to children that they can interpret these instructions in their own way. They like to conform. They try desperately to be the same as everybody else and not stand out from the crowd.

Imagine children who find it takes them longer physically to write the words than others in their class working to the instruction that the work must be finished by playtime. They will make their piece of work extremely short so that it gets completed on time. The result of this might be, '*Is this all you've managed to do?*'

The child who's asked to write about Saturday but who didn't do anything exciting on Saturday will write about a boring day. The teacher, who wants a 'good story' back will say, '*Couldn't you write something more exciting?*'.

Asked to write about their birthday party – if they had one they'll write a true piece about it. If they didn't, they'll sit and chew their pencil for half an hour because they don't like to admit they didn't have one and they don't think it's acceptable to *make it up* – '*Is that all you've done in half an hour?*'.

Of course, lots of teachers recognise these problems, and make allowances for them.

Time limits probably affect the writing most. Some children think quickly, some think slowly. Some children find the physical act of wielding the pen so easy they can manage pages of A4 whilst others are still on the third line when the bell goes.

If *you* are still on the third line and the bell goes and the books are collected in for marking exactly how true will the assessment of your product – and thus your ability – be? And how far is your piece of work an act of *com*position or an act of *im*position? Has it come from you, from your imagination? Or has it come really from the set of constraints that were inflicted on it?

How Do Children Improve Their Writing?

Somehow, through all this confusion of instruction and pressure, of trying to learn conventions and remember spellings and the rules of grammar, of worrying about handwriting and what it is the teacher really wants – somehow, despite all of this, children's writing skills do develop. How does it happen?

You might think that children learn because when they get their work back and it's marked they take note of all the points where they went wrong and put them right the next time.

But, of course, the next time they write the constraints are the same or similar. Even if they have taken any notice of the red pen marks on their books they are not likely to remember them and carry them in their heads during the act of writing a new piece of work because, if they did, how would they concentrate on what they're writing now?

The simple fact of writing is that it is a process that *develops*, just as other skills develop. The more you do it, the better you get at it. The more highly motivated you are to do it, the more progress you make. The more you *want* to do it, the more you will cultivate the skills involved in it.

An Experiment To Help You Understand Your Child's Writing Skills

You can get a very good idea of what your children's real abilities in writing are, by intervening in the process.

Ask or encourage them to do a piece of writing by themselves. You need to be a bit canny about this. Your aim is to end up with a piece of work that you can evaluate but don't tell them this. Think of a writing activity that might be interesting to them – writing a letter to someone, relating a family event, writing a story about something they've seen on television. The content idea itself doesn't matter as long as it is fairly stimulating for them.

Supply paper, pens or pencils, space and time. Then get busy with something else so that you can't disturb them. They should not be given any assistance or help from anyone. When they've finished, collect what they've written, read it and praise them. Then keep it somewhere safe. You will need it to compare with the next piece of writing.

Leave a day or two, then suggest another piece of writing. This time, sit with them. Before they even begin to put pen to paper, talk about whatever the content idea is. For example, if it's a letter to Granny ask them, *'What would she be interested in hearing about? How can we make her feel pleased to get our letter? What should we ask her about her own life?'* etc. etc. Have a general discussion about the contents and presentation of the letter. In other words, plan it together. Stay sitting with them while they write. When they get stuck on spellings, grammar or ideas, help. Remind them about points they want to put in the letter. Generally intervene wherever you can but in a helpful way not a negative way.

Try to let them see that you are there as a support, not a critic.

UNDERSTANDING YOUR CHILD'S THOUGHT PROCESSES

While you're making this intervention you will get a good idea of the thought processes your children are using when they are writing. You'll find out how often they come up against words they're not sure how to spell and you'll find out what their strategies for coping with this are. Do they instantly decide on a simpler word? Do they reach for a dictionary? Do they simply ask you how to spell it?

The same goes for punctuation and grammar. They might be writing away and suddenly ask you, '*Should I put a question mark here?*' If you were not there to help, what would they do?

* Forget it altogether?
* Change the sentence?
* Put the question mark anyway?

Whatever happens, at the end of the writing, collect the product, read through it together, let them make any corrections they want to make, and praise them for their work. Keep the product.

EVALUATING THE TWO PIECES

Now comes the fun part. You need to look at both pieces of work, side by side.

How much difference is there in

* length?
* spelling?
* content?
* grammar?
* confidence?
* handwriting?

You will probably be very surprised. Usually there are huge differences. The point is, which piece of work demonstrates the writer's real ability – the piece with no outside intervention, or the piece with?

There are two schools of thought here. One school has it that what the writer can do alone, without any help from anyone or anything, is what the writer is really capable of. After all, in exams the pupil is always alone.

The second school has it that, since writing is a process of development, leading the writer to 'do better' is an enabling factor that helps progress. It's a kind of 'sitting next to Nellie' way of learning. The apprentice writer picks up skills and refines them with the help of the expert.

How much do you think your own abilities in any activity would improve if you had an expert at the side of you as you worked, helping and encouraging, answering your queries, showing you the way? Would you appreciate this as a good way of learning?

Isn't it true that the more you support and assist the

children to develop their own thought processes, then the more ability they will have once they are left to their own devices?

Practical Activities

SET UP A WRITING CORNER
Set up a writing corner somewhere in the house. It needn't be huge, but it needs to be away from other distractions as much as possible. Try to get it out of viewing distance of the television, and away from the toy corner that might claim their interests!

Furnish the corner with a box of writing paper of different sizes, shapes, colours, thicknesses and a box of writing implements – pencils, pens, felts, crayons, chalks. Most children adore stationery so if you can run to bits and pieces like one or two folders, bulldog clips, paper clips, rubber bands, a stapler, and a large notice board with coloured pins to stick work to, so much the better! You could instigate a 'Piece of writing of the week!' notice so that something new got pinned up for the whole family to read, every week.

WRITING TASKS
You can try the following kinds of writing task with children of any age at any stage of development. Little children will enjoy drawing the picture first and having you help them write down the words they want to say. Give them the opportunity to copy and trace your words whenever they want to. Ask your child to do the following, for instance:

* Write a shopping list.
* Write a list of things you would love to have if you could have anything you wanted.
* Write a letter to a member of the family or a friend.
* Write a fan letter to someone on TV, movies, videos, or someone whose books you really like.
* Write a poem about something that makes you sad.
* Write a poem about something that makes you happy.
* Write new words to your favourite nursery rhyme/song.
* Write the story of a story that you've read and enjoyed.
* Make up a story about you and a friend having an adventure together.
* Look for word fridge magnets that you can use on the fridge to make a new poem every day.

Chapter Four

THE DIFFICULTIES OF WRITING AND HOW YOU CAN HELP

WHAT MAKES WRITING SO HARD?

The complexity of writing and children's lack of confidence are the two biggest difficulties. As with any skills that children are developing, what they *feel* about what they're doing makes all the difference to *how* they do it. Often children view writing as a very difficult task right from the moment they understand the problem of having to get it 'right'.

WRITING INVOLVES MANY SKILLS

With reading it's quite possible to get the meaning of a text and be able to read it even if you can't quite get the finest details right. But with writing there is always the anxiety of having to have every single bit correct, otherwise other people might not understand it. Not only that – but people have to be able to read it, so it has to be extra tidy!

Children who are often told that their handwriting is untidy sometimes come to believe that the criticism also applies to the content. Many children grow up thinking that if their handwriting is not very good then they are not very good writers, they aren't knowledgeable, and they cannot write clearly in terms of their content. Often as adults they will say, '*Oh, I can't write anything!*' when all they really need to do is improve their handwriting or use a word processor!

THINKING OF SOMETHING TO WRITE ABOUT

Very often, at the point of writing, children say, '*I can't think of anything to write*'. What they usually mean is one of four things:

1. 'Writing is a meaningless chore that is only for the teacher's benefit (to keep the children quiet and occupied).'

2. 'When I write I make loads of mistakes which have to be marked. Then I feel really thick.'

3. 'For writing you have to have good ideas and a creative mind, and I haven't got either.'

4. 'What is the point of writing anyway – when nobody will take any notice of what I've written?'

If, as an interested parent, you can pre-empt these attitudes before they even begin to get a hold, then you have given your children the best start to writing that you possibly can.

If children are highly motivated to get their ideas down before they lose them – never mind *how* until after the ideas are captured – then they are likely to put in their very best effort and enjoy doing so, without even thinking about it.

Helping Your Child To Be Positive Towards Writing

Make sure you are positive about writing so you dispel all their worries.

WRITING FOR THE FUN OF IT
'Writing is a meaningless chore done for the teacher's benefit.'
You need to give children the feeling that writing is something they are free to do for the love of it. Once they have learned this feeling as little children, it will stay with them for ever no matter what happens in school.

Children will always model themselves on what happens around them, particularly in the home. So, just as it is never too early to begin 'reading' with children, it is also never too early to begin 'writing'.

More often than not, children's skills in writing will be well behind their skills in speaking. This doesn't mean that they can't observe and understand what you are doing when you are in the act of writing.

The more they see you picking up a pen or pencil and scribbling notes, writing letters, jotting down little stories or ideas, the more they will get the idea that this is a good and natural thing to do.

Talk to them while you're writing – *'Let's send Granny a letter and tell her where we went today,' 'Draw me a picture of the park and we'll send it to Grandad with some writing on to tell him what we did'* – etc.

Writing captions to photographs in albums is an

especially good activity. Involve the children themselves – *'What shall we write for this one?'* – and encourage them to tell you their anecdotes. Repeat the words as you write them down. Encourage them to copy or trace the writing if they show interest in doing so.

Read the writing back and ask them if it's what they wanted to say. Sometimes they want to 'pretend' read the words – help them to do this with lots of encouragement and praise.

You can also point out things like the capital letter that begins their name – *'See? "T" for Tom!'* and words and phrases like *'love from'* which occur regularly and often.

Many children build up a bank of 'whole words' to write when they begin writing, in much the same way as they build up a bank of 'whole words' to read when they begin reading. Lots of repetition helps this facility to develop.

DON'T WORRY ABOUT THE MISTAKES
'When I write I make loads of mistakes which have to be marked. Then I feel really thick.'

If you can teach your children that writing is not something they are expected to be able to do perfectly, right from the beginning and that they will learn how to do it as they go along, then they will be a long way towards negating this attitude.

The way to do this, is to teach them very carefully and very positively.

Most children, when they begin writing, keep

asking for someone to show them the words or spell the words out for them. Give them the confidence to have a go for themselves.

If they say, *'How do you spell "Granny"?'*, say, *'You could probably do it yourself if you had a go. What do you think it starts with?'* and help them to get the 'g' down. Next, say, *'Listen to the word. G-r-anny. What do you think might come next?'* and so on, until they have done it for themselves, with just a bit of help.

By doing this you will help them to build the confidence they need to be able to tackle new words later on without resorting to using another word in preference or changing the sentence to eliminate it altogether.

When they begin to write they may ask you, *'Is this right?'* – and how you answer will colour their ideas about their ability. For instance, if you say, *'No, you've spelt that word wrong. And this is how you do this letter, not like that!'* in a cross kind of voice, then you are going to reinforce the idea that they are failing.

In fact, if you take a developmental view of writing, children cannot be 'failing' at all, for they are not born knowing how to write and then getting it wrong. They are born as 'clean slates' and develop the skills of writing that they need to be fluent and accurate, as they go along.

Correct them in a very positive way. For example, if they have spelled the word 'friend' wrong, instead of jumping on them for a wrong spelling, say, *'You got the "f" and the "r" right, and the "nd", well done. But we need to do something about the rest of it. What do you think we might do?'*

If they have no idea then just tell them, simply, without any fuss, *'Friend is spelt f-r-i-e-n-d,'* and get them to cross out the word and write the correct spelling in its place.

Make sure they understand that looking at spelling and handwriting is something everyone needs to do after they have finished getting the message down. Some mistakes happen because, even though we know how to spell words, our brains are so busy concentrating on what we want to say that we write down the wrong word or get the letters in the wrong order. Sometimes we are writing so fast that words that sound the same as the words we want to use (homophones) are written in their place (for instance their/there, bare/bear, our/are).

Give them the idea of 'reviewing' their writing, right from the beginning, simply by reading back whatever you have written yourself, or together, and commenting on it. This way they will feel it is part of the natural process of writing and it will hold no fear for them.

EVERYDAY EVENTS ARE BRILLIANT IDEAS TO WRITE ABOUT

'For writing you have to have good ideas and a creative mind, and I haven't got either.'

When children feel that teachers expect them to come up with brilliant ideas all the time, they are soon put off trying. In actual fact, all they really need to do is to look at the world through their own eyes and write about it.

In the adult world every experience we have is

assimilated into our normal pattern of behaviour or thinking – everything is added to what we already know. In a child's world everything is new and therefore all awareness is heightened. Their lives stretch out before them, a voyage of discovery – everything is different, everything is exciting.

Their stories and messages can convey that excitement as long as they are allowed to write from their own point of view and are not pushed into writing from an adult point of view.

They may write, *'The snow feels all shivery and tingly'* and the adult may say, *'That doesn't make sense!'* but to the child it does make sense because the world is all about feeling. When he tries to describe the snow he *is* the snow.

From the outset, try to give your children the freedom to write as they feel. Allow them to have a crack at what they want to say, encourage them to put all their effort into finding the meaning in what they want to say so that they don't feel hemmed in by 'trying to make sense' or 'writing sensible things'.

The more they are allowed to express their own ideas and feelings in their early days of writing, the less inhibitions they will have later on when they are expected to display creative ideas. Basically, you are encouraging confidence so that the children will always be secure enough in their ideas – no matter how way out they may be! – to take the risk of writing them down on paper.

BE A 'WIDER AUDIENCE' FOR YOUR CHILD
'What is the point of writing it anyway – when nobody will take any notice of what I've written?'

A huge and very real offputting problem in school is that, although children may write several times a day, every day, nobody gets to see it except the teacher who 'marks' it.

The nature of every kind of writing is the expectation that it will be read by an audience. Sometimes the reader may simply be the writer – in the case of shopping lists, therapeutic writing, etc. But children often need a much wider audience if they are not to become bored with the whole thing.

School tradition has been for 'good work' to be displayed on the wall. Even that can be offputting to some children, who very often compare themselves with others in their class and compare themselves badly. It's even worse if only the 'best' work gets displayed and some children never see their work on the wall, though this happens less often these days as most teachers are aware of the problems.

The result is that children won't strive to make their work 'good enough to go on the wall' because they don't want it to be side by side with the 'best work' of someone with greater skill, when theirs will pale into insignificance.

Many teachers today try to 'publish' children's work rather than put it on display to invite comparison. They do this by using folders rather than exercise books; by getting children to 'make books' rather than just write compositions; by binding together 'anthologies' of children's poetry and stories, rather than having each child's work separately in their own books.

These strategies mean that other children in the class or school, and other adults, can read the children's work, not to criticise and mark it, but to enjoy it as reading material.

Unfortunately time and resources often make this quite a difficult thing to do in the classroom. But it's something you can do very easily and cheaply at home. All you are aiming at is putting the children's writing on show so that other people can read it. Ideas for 'publishing' are given in the Practical Activities section of this chapter.

HELP YOUR CHILD DEAL WITH 'MARKING'

The traditional way of working in school is that children write, teachers mark. Many teachers feel that unless they indicate every single error that a child makes, with a red pen, then they are not doing their job. In fact, parents have been known to leap upon unmarked spelling mistakes or syntactical errors on Parents' Nights as evidence of a teacher not bothering with their child's work.

The psychological problems for the child, with this kind of marking, are many.

A child who is having trouble mastering the rules of grammar will not be inspired by a returned exercise book covered with red pen. In fact the reverse will be true. The child will be totally discouraged. A child who is having difficulties with spelling and punctuation will not learn to improve at all by being faced with the huge number of errors that have been made in one piece of work. It will, simply, all be too much.

In fact, children whose work is marked and shown to be lacking will very quickly lose confidence and motivation!

If this is how your child's teacher marks the work, take all the opportunities you can to get into a discussion with the child about it. It's difficult because you cannot be seen to criticise the teacher as the child may lose respect for her. However, you need to be able to guide the child to see something positive in the system of marking. Suggest that you work together on some of the problems, taking them one at a time, and help the child to master them slowly.

Remember that spelling, grammar and punctuation are all learned in a developmental way, rather as walking and talking are.

The rules can be taught at all different stages of writing development. They may have to be repeated many times, over a long period of time before they are fully assimilated. Repetition of the rules will help the child eventually to begin to see the light.

Often, if you study your child's errors, you can analyse their method of building understanding. The errors will show you what your child understands about letters and sounds, and what they don't. Rather than giving the accusatory red pen mark it is better to analyse what the next point of learning might be, and work on it.

There is another point to be made here. Parents often feel secure when their children's school is teaching in the same way that they were taught, as though, if *they* learned by that method, then their children will also. This, of course, is not always true – and anyhow, who is to say that the parent may not have learned more easily if a different method had been used?

One of the traditional ways of marking 'composition' was to give points out of ten. This appeared to work quite well but there is now a substantial amount of evidence pointing to the fact that if rewards or tokens are given for an activity, then the activity is less likely to be undertaken freely and voluntarily when the reward is withdrawn.

In other words, children who are bribed with pocket money to wash up are very unlikely ever to wash up without the prospect of being paid for it! Likewise, if rewards (marks) are given for a piece of written work, then the activity of writing is very unlikely ever to be embarked upon and enjoyed just for its own sake.

What really needs to happen is for the developing writer to be given some experience of internal satisfaction and achievement – then, in the act of writing, the writer will always aspire to reconstruct those feelings. You can give your children such a wonderful feeling with some of the practical activities that follow.

PRACTICAL ACTIVITIES

SURROUND YOUR CHILD WITH LITERATURE
All children need stories, rhymes, poetry, ideas. Children who are going to write need them even more.

They need to hear, read and talk about literature with you, with other children, and other adults.

Literature gives them a good model for writing. It shows them that when people write they use a different voice, almost a different kind of language, from the voice they use to speak with. It gives them models from which they will be able to compose their own pieces of writing.

From reading lots of different literature, children learn all about drama and problem-solving and about how to make writing 'come alive'.

SHARED WRITING

Sharing writing with your children is an exciting way to communicate with them. It can be quite time-consuming, but there really isn't any need to make it so. Embark upon the activity as a game you play together, with an attitude of pleasure and excitement, rather than seeing it as *'Helping the children to learn to write'*!

You need to have a book and writing implements. If your children are very young I would suggest a large A4 size note or sketch book, without lines.

Cover the book with some decorative paper, or a picture or photograph they particularly like. Give your book a name 'Our Book', 'Journal', 'Mine and Yours' – whatever you think will appeal. Even better – choose the title together.

The idea is that each of you write in the book, passing messages to each other. The writing in this book is purely about *message* – correcting spellings and punctuation or anything like that has absolutely no place in it!

Start the writing yourself. Write a message on the first page – it can be anything you like, but try to write something that will get a response. For instance, *'I really enjoyed the party today. I loved the birthday cake. The games were good fun. Which did you like best?'* Illustrate your page of writing if you feel like it.

Leave the book somewhere for your child to read it and respond. Don't make any rules about where or when. Make it a completely free activity.

If your child is not yet a reader, read the page aloud and write down the response yourself, demonstrating how the words are written. Read back what they have said.

When your child has responded, write another page. It may be a continuation of the same topic, or you may need to write something different. You need to judge what you think will capture the child's interest.

Once the habit has formed, the shared book will become a strong piece of communication between you. Often you find that children tell you things in the shared book that they wouldn't dare to tell you with their voices. Sometimes they try to work out problems with you that are too difficult for them to talk about. Sometimes they just enjoy the security of having a 'secret' way of communicating between you. You might be surprised to find how much you enjoy the activity too!

Even if your children are very young, encourage them to take part. They can draw pictures to convey their messages. You can read to them, in a whisper, the words that you have written. As they learn to write, so their contributions will develop.

Although the book is about message, occasionally the children may ask you if they have made mistakes with their spellings or grammar. This probably means that they are ready to learn so encourage them as much as you can. As long as they have come to you for help, rather than you criticising them, you cannot go far wrong!

This kind of shared writing can actually last for as long as you want it to. However, it's best to keep the books themselves quite short – not too many pages!

When a book is full, agree a place where you will keep it. You can look back at your library of shared writing as your children are growing up and they – and you – will be amazed at their progress! It often helps children to look back at their work in this way. They like to see the wibbly wobbly writing they did as infants, and the silly mistakes they made! It boosts their confidence in their progress.

PUBLISHING WRITING

You can publish the children's writing, of course, by sticking it on the kitchen wall for everyone to see! You could have a special Story Wall or Story Board. Cover it with brightly coloured paper and give the children the opportunity to display all forms of writing on it.

If you are encouraging your children to write stories, poems, or write about trips that you have made or things you have done together, instead of giving them an exercise book to write in, get them to make books.

For some reason 'making books' is always seen as a much more exciting activity than 'writing a story' even though the task may be the same! There is a kind of magic about it for children of every age, at every stage of writing, and it is something I have never found them to get bored with!

All you need for 'making books' is some sheets of plain paper for the writing, card for the covers, and something to fix the books together. This can be sellotape, staples, ribbon, wool or steel rings through punched holes, etc.

The pages need to be written individually first, then the illustrations done. Often it helps if the illustrations are done on plain paper, cut out and stuck on to the written pages so that if the children aren't happy about their pictures they don't have to do the writing all over again.

The covers should be illustrated and titled. Most children enjoy writing an inside page 'About the Author' and a blurb on the back page which gives a synopsis of the book.

Your books can be as simple or as complex as the children want them to be. Supply brightly coloured card and felt tip pens for all the decorative bits. Often you can persuade the children to draw margins round the pages and do writing patterns in them – this is all grist to the handwriting mill!

You can make 'shape' books by cutting the card and the inside pages into the shape of something concerned with the topic – for example cut them into the shape of a football if the topic is a visit to a football match.

Another, simpler (but not so much fun!) way to

publish is to invest in a lever-arch file and fill it with plastic folders. The stories, poems, books can be inserted into the folders. They might be labelled with names and dates for even more interest. The children will love looking back at them and so will other members of the family.

Chapter Five

LEARNING THE RULES OF WRITING

At some point children have to learn about:

* Grammar
* Punctuation
* Spelling
* Handwriting

Spelling and punctuation, in particular, are huge obstacles for many children. So much so that if they want to use a word that's difficult for them to spell, they'll use an easy word instead. If they're not sure of the punctuation marks they'd like to use, they'll put a simple full stop.

GRAMMAR

WHY GRAMMAR IS SO DIFFICULT TO LEARN

The Concept Of A Sentence.
Until children really understand the idea of a sentence they will not be able to write in a grammatical form and then other people (readers) may not be able to

understand their message. However, a sentence is an extremely hard concept for children to understand.

The usual way of explaining 'sentence' is that it is a group of words beginning with a capital letter, ending with a full stop and making sense. But what on earth can such an explanation mean to a child? After all, they know that lots of things make sense to adults that don't make any sense whatsoever to them!

There are several ways to get the idea of a sentence across to children.

(i) Read aloud, often and regularly, using the punctuation marks as places to pause. Point out to them where a sentence begins and ends. Show that it has a capital letter at the beginning, and a full stop at the end. Why do they think this is so?

(ii) Play sentence games where you and the children choose words for each other to put into a sentence. Turn it into a fun game by giving points for right answers – call the points 'bananas' or 'strawberries'.

(iii) It's the repetition that gets the idea finally lodged in the brain, so don't be afraid to do it over and over again.

We Don't Always Use Good Grammar When We Speak.
When we talk we use a kind of shorthand most of the time. We don't finish sentences – sometimes we don't even begin them properly. We certainly don't speak in 'proper' sentences : *'We went...', '...going shopping!' 'Because I said so!'*

Because children base their writing on speech, they tend to make the same mistakes over and over again. For example they will write, *'I would of gone...' 'I might of said it...' 'He shouldn't of been late...'* or, even, *'woulda', shouldn'ta', 'mighta'*, because what they *hear* is 'of' or 'a' instead of 'have' and it doesn't occur to them to wonder whether it makes sense or not.

In the early stages of writing, the child's grammar will always model the way they use language in other forms of communication. You can only really change it by pointing out that other people (readers) will not understand the message because while what they are saying sounds more or less all right in speech, it doesn't make sense in writing. You then have to tell the child how to put it right.

Constant repetition of specific mistakes will ensure that the child eventually gets the message. This is not to say that you should swoop on every mistake. Much better to adopt an attitude of calm and say, *'What can you notice that might be wrong with this sentence?'*

HOW GRAMMAR IS TAUGHT IN SCHOOLS

Grammar Exercises
In the past children did grammar exercises over and over again, to practise a particular concept. They had to answer questions, ticking the right box, choosing the correct word, etc.

Research showed that, although the children learned to pick the right answer, in the majority of instances the learning and knowledge was not transferred to a functional use. In other words, although if asked (for example) to:

> *Tick the right box:*
> *I could (of) (have) gone.*

the children might tick 'have' ten times out of ten, when it came to free composition or story-writing, the possibility was always that they would write 'I could of done that'.

It's difficult to get into children's minds to see what and how they are thinking, but it's quite possible that some children acquired the idea that 'have' only applied to grammar exercises and not to functional writing or speech.

Learning Grammar Through Writing
More recently, the trend was for grammar not to be taught in isolation, but for points to be highlighted or focused upon during reading and writing activities. Many primary school children did not really have any formal grammar teaching

Combining The Two Methods
Today's favoured way of teaching grammar is to combine the two methods: children are taught the parts of speech and rules of grammar and then how to put it to a functional use.

It means that while children are writing the teacher will be pointing out a particular rule of grammar, so that the writer pays particular attention to it, and hopefully learns it. So that, for example, as in the above case, the teacher would look at the writing and would say, *'Is "of" the right word here? What do we normally say? What is the word that we should say?'*

PUNCTUATION

Punctuation is a set of marks that breaks words into groups so that their meaning is clear. When someone speaks they make the meaning of their words clear with intonation, pauses, gestures. They can vary the speed and tone of their voice and use expression. We can't do that in writing, so we use punctuation marks instead.

FULL STOPS
Punctuation often becomes a major battle for many children. At the first stages of writing children sometimes completely misunderstand the concept of putting in capital letters and full stops. Often they will present work where the beginning of every line has a capital letter, the end of every line has a full stop. (I was baffled by the work of one child who began every single sentence: *A. the . . . A. she. . . A. nobody. . .* until it finally dawned on me that when I said that every sentence began with 'a capital letter', he understood *'a (vowel sound) – capital letter'*, therefore every sentence began with A. *'Full stop at the end. . .'* to him meant at the end of the capital A.)

Sometimes children will leave the full stops out altogether rather than put them in the wrong place. Others will put them in like peas through a pea-shooter, dotting them about at will.

If they are doing this they have still not understood the concept of a sentence, so you have to keep working on it with sentence games and using other reading material as a model.

QUESTION MARKS

The next easiest punctuation mark to understand is the question mark. It's easy because by this time the children know what a sentence is and can usually understand the intonation of a spoken question.

Often, even though they understand the concept, they forget to put the question mark in, but gentle probing about what they've written (*'Do you think that's a question? Or not? What do you think should be at the end of it then?'*) can usually give them a nudge in the right direction.

SPEECH MARKS

Speech marks usually come next and, contrary to expectation, they're often assimilated quite easily. This is partly due to the fact that children understand about speech bubbles in comic strips. If they are taught to use speech bubbles and then to use speech marks, they pick up the idea very easily. The Practical Activities at the end of this chapter will give you some examples of what to do.

APOSTROPHES

After speech marks, punctuation tends to get more difficult. The apostrophe denoting ownership and the apostrophe denoting a shortened word often get muddled up. Worse – once the children have come across apostrophes they tend to think they can put them in whenever they see an 's' at the end of a word!

COMMAS
The comma is particularly difficult to understand, until children have some idea of clauses. This doesn't always develop until the later stages of writing, but it is well worth taking younger writers through the various rules. Even though they may not assimilate all of them, they will learn some. A good way to start is to suggest to children that they read through their work, and if they pause in the middle of a sentence, put a comma in there.

HELPING YOUR CHILD WITH PUNCTUATION
The crucial thing to remember is that it is really not worth working on more than one punctuation mark at a time. All you will do is confuse the children utterly, and probably put them off! Try to take one point at a time and work on it, reinforcing it until your child begins to use it correctly.

Give lots of praise as a reward for learning, and don't be too eager to move on to the next punctuation mark. Leave a breathing space so that the child can really learn one punctuation mark before embarking upon the next one.

As with all teaching and learning, time, patience and repetition are the keys.

SPELLING

Many, many children can learn words to reproduce exactly during the traditional spelling test, but then cannot get them right in a functional piece of work.

Learning to spell is important to writing, not least because once the children are fairly confident with spelling they can focus on their message and content. It is one less thing to worry about.

Children understand that spelling needs to be good because it is 'what the reader sees'. Many, many adults have been put down, or put themselves down, as poor writers when, in fact, their content is extremely good. It is only the spelling that needs attention.

FIRST ATTEMPTS AT SPELLING

When children begin to compose and write in recognisable letters they rely mostly on consonants. The consonant sounds are easier for them to hear and recognise than vowel sounds. They will write things like:

SSKtN (this is a kitten)

though they may not be able to remember what it says after a few minutes. You can see where the sounds come from and how they have been formed to make the sentence – it's all fairly logical!

Sometimes they will use the initial sounds, sometimes the ending, sometimes a middle sound.

ASKING FOR HELP

Over a period of time, with help, children want to be able to spell correctly and this is when they begin to ask you for spellings.

If they are too anxious they will come to you for every word. You then have to ask yourself, *'How much of this writing is theirs, how much is mine?'* Encourage

LEARNING THE RULES OF WRITING

them to 'have a go' at the word they want rather than just giving them the spelling, as this will actually help them to evolve their own ability to spell.

Help them to work out which sounds they can hear in the words, and in which order they come. But remember that children's auditory discrimination is not so developed as adults'. Therefore they may not hear some sounds, for example the 'n' in 'went'.

Praise them for the letters and sounds that they get right, and help them to spot any missing letters or sounds by going through the words carefully and slowly.

HOW SPELLING IS TAUGHT IN SCHOOLS

In the past, children would 'line up' at the teacher's desk for spellings of words to write their stories. This meant that they would get a word, go back to their place and write it, then want another word so join the queue again. It was common to have twenty-odd children all lined up at a time and it meant that most of the children spent most of the writing lesson lined up at the teacher's desk, rather than on the task! They certainly weren't learning to compose with such gaps of time being wasted between each word!

Today, children are expected and encouraged to try to work out the spelling for themselves, using auditory clues and knowledge that they have about letter sounds, and from using personal word books that they've built up with the teacher.

INVENTED SPELLING

To start with children begin to use what teachers call 'invented' spelling. They use all the knowledge at their command to work out how they think words should really be spelt.

There are clear stages to 'invented spelling' and over a period of a few weeks it is quite possible to see clear progress. For example 'lc' might be invented for 'luck', progressing through 'loc' to 'lok' to 'luk' to 'luck'. 'Went' might begin as 'wt', go through 'wnt' and 'wnet', progressing to 'went'.

Often, words look completely unreadable at first glance – '*fllowz, esspt, breth*' – but when you really break it down, you can see that what is written is quite a logical way of spelling 'flowers, except, breathe'.

HOW CHILDREN THEMSELVES LEARN TO SPELL

Spelling, as we've seen above, is not just about hearing. It is also about visual memory – being able to 'see' in the mind the way the words are formed – and about the movement of the arm and hand in making the letters. The more the hand gets used to making the shape of the word, the more a pathway is formed in the brain that helps children remember the spelling.

Children need to build up a broad repertoire of spelling strategies to help them. The Practical Activities section at the end of this chapter gives lots of ideas for use with your children.

WHAT PROBLEMS DO CHILDREN HAVE WITH SPELLING?

Different children present different problems with spelling and those different problems need a different kind of handling.

(i) Children who are perfectionists are usually intelligent. They know that words are only spelled one way. They are fearful of making errors, because errors will make their self esteem plummet. They will sit with a pencil and not write until the teacher has given them the spelling of the word they want, no matter how long it takes. They cannot bear to take risks by inventing their spellings.

These children need encouragement to move on, to invent the words they don't know the proper spelling for, and to check them later with someone, or something, who does. If they don't learn how to do this in the early stages of writing, they will always be held back, their writing blocked by the fear of getting it wrong.

(ii) On the other hand, some children protest that even though there may be a lot of words to be corrected in a piece of writing, they will not do a new draft because they 'know what it says'. Basically these writers have misunderstood the fine balance between message and medium.

These children can be helped by you pointing out that their work would be good to publish, because of its message, but other people might not be able to understand it because of the spelling mistakes so – *'Could we put them right first, do you think?'*

(iii) Some writers haven't a good self-image as spellers. When they get to a word they want to write that seems just a little bit too hard to invent or look up, they find an easy word to use instead, even if it spoils the meaning. The struggle is too much for them, so they don't try.

These children can be helped by lots of encouragement. *'Oh, "hospital" would have been a good word to use there or "ambulance". Let's see if we can spell it together.'*

(iv) Children who tell themselves they can't spell, very often never learn to spell very well because, as with everything else, *'I can't...'* becomes a self-fulfilling prophesy. Sometimes they will make their writing so slow that they hardly produce anything at all. Often they can do quite well in spelling tests, but because they have poor visual and auditory memories they become very weak spellers when writing.

You can help these children by giving them the chance to understand their problems. You need to go through the spelling rules with them and help them to build up dictionaries and word lists that will be useful to them. They need to know how to look at their work and try to estimate which words might be difficult. Build up their confidence in any way you can whenever an opportunity arises.

HANDWRITING

Handwriting is all about large muscle control, fine muscle control, and hand and eye co-ordination.

The development of handwriting usually follows five stages, all of which overlap.

THE STAGES OF DEVELOPING HANDWRITING

(i) The first stage is when the writers are anxious to get whatever they can get down on paper, regardless of what it looks like. They usually scrawl all across the pages, quite happily. It doesn't take long for them to understand that the writing generally goes from left to right, though they may not take much notice of the spacing of letters, or the fact that there need to be spaces between words.

(ii) After a while, children begin to appreciate what the writing *looks* like. They like to work on a 'clean' page, without any smudges or marks. At this point they may get quite cross with any mistakes they make and try to rub them out – often putting so much effort into their erasing that they rub right through the paper!

(iii) Next, the children become quite fussy about the spacing between words, and about writing on lines or just above or below lines. At this point, the inner critic begins to take over a little, and slows down the composition to make the handwriting more pleasing to the writer.

(iv) After this, developing writers either decide their handwriting is 'no good' and therefore they can't write, i.e. have nothing to say, or they work at developing their handwriting as they develop their composing skills.

HOW HANDWRITING AFFECTS COMPOSITION OR MESSAGE

If a writer has lots to say and is totally confident in saying it, then, during the composition, the handwriting critic will probably be 'switched off' as the message takes precedence.

If handwriting becomes an issue that stands alone, two kinds of problem can result. The first is that a writer with good handwriting will believe the information it conveys is as clear as the handwriting. The other is that a writer whose handwriting is felt to be untidy or unacceptable, will feel the content is unacceptable as well.

LOCATING PROBLEM AREAS

Sometimes developing writers have problems with all areas of these conventions, sometimes with only one or another.

In order to help your children, you need to decide, if there is a problem area or more than one, which has the most priority, and work on them one at a time.

Children sometimes think that parents helping at home are an interference and an imposition. They're frightened that what you do is not 'what we do in school'. Try to break through this barrier by showing them that all support is good support, and all experience adds to what they learn in school. If it *is* different, then maybe that's a help because it gives another way of looking at a problem. No one method is wrong or right, just different.

GETTING SAMPLES OF WRITING TO COMPARE

To find out where your children are having problems with writing and, if they are, what those problems are, you need to take a fair sample of pieces of writing, not just look at one.

Try to get the children to write at different times of the day or week, on different topics, in different ways. Get them to write a varied assortment of story, poem, letter, information, etc. and try to gauge the kind of mood they are in when they do it because this will help you to analyse how valid a piece of work it is.

Obviously if they are always tired from a day at school then you are not going to get their best efforts so try to get them writing when they have a clear mind and are full of energy.

Analyse the different pieces of writing carefully. The handwriting may not always match. The spelling might be better one day than another. Try to work out what makes a good day, what makes a bad day – and what difference that makes to the writing.

DEALING WITH YOUR CHILD'S WORRIES

Ask the children themselves if they worry about their writing and, if so, what features worry them most. If they could have lots of help and support which of the conventions would they choose to work on first? They are the writers, after all, and are probably aware of their limitations. Even if those limitations are false notions you can help to dispel them with a bit of positive encouragement.

Often, you will find that exercises do help. With repetitive exercises, everything depends on your approach. If they think the work is going to be boring and humdrum then it will be. You have to try and find fun ways of getting into it. You can buy all kinds of books and sheets that you can work on with the children, to help boost their confidence. Remember, at all times, the notion of transference – it is crucial that the children transfer the knowledge they have acquired from the exercises, into their functional writing.

This kind of support at home often breaks down problems that seem insurmountable to the child at school. The magic ingredient, of course, is usually the one to one attention that they will get from you.

Confusing Normal Stages Of Development With Real Problems

Everything is relative, and in a classroom of thirty-plus children it's practically impossible for a teacher to give everyone independent instruction about everything. There's often a desperate struggle to bring the poorest in the class up to scratch with the average. Quiet children, especially, tend to fall through the net because they don't make a fuss about what they see as their problems. Often they don't feel that they're entitled to any personal help. Also, they sometimes try to hide their worries and anxieties, hoping that their difficulties will resolve themselves. Often, of course, they do.

Not every child who has untidy handwriting, or poor spelling development, has dyslexia. In fact, most problems are not problems at all but stages of development that disappear as skills are practised. Children develop different skills at different rates. Be aware of this, and try to keep an open mind, but if you are really worried about your children's development then do not lose any time in making an appointment to discuss it with the teacher.

PRACTICAL ACTIVITIES

REINFORCING GRAMMAR
* Give the children good models of speech and literature at all times. The more you talk and read to them, the better their writing will be.

* Play sentence games. You give a sentence, they give a sentence in return. You give a phrase, they try and turn it into a sentence. You give a word, they try to turn it into a sentence.

* Together, make 'silly sentence' books. You need two sheets of white A4 paper at least, and some card for a cover. Fold the A4 sheets so that the short edges meet. Cut along the middle to make four separate sheets. Draw a line 2 cm from the left-hand long edge of each sheet. Fold the paper backwards and forwards along these lines. Draw four equally spaced lines down the pages. Write a sentence along each page with a thick felt-tip. Glue the pages together along the 2 cm margin. When the glue is dry cut along the four drawn lines to the margin. Glue or staple the cover to the pages. Flip over the sections to make silly sentences. (See Fig.1.)

Fig. 1

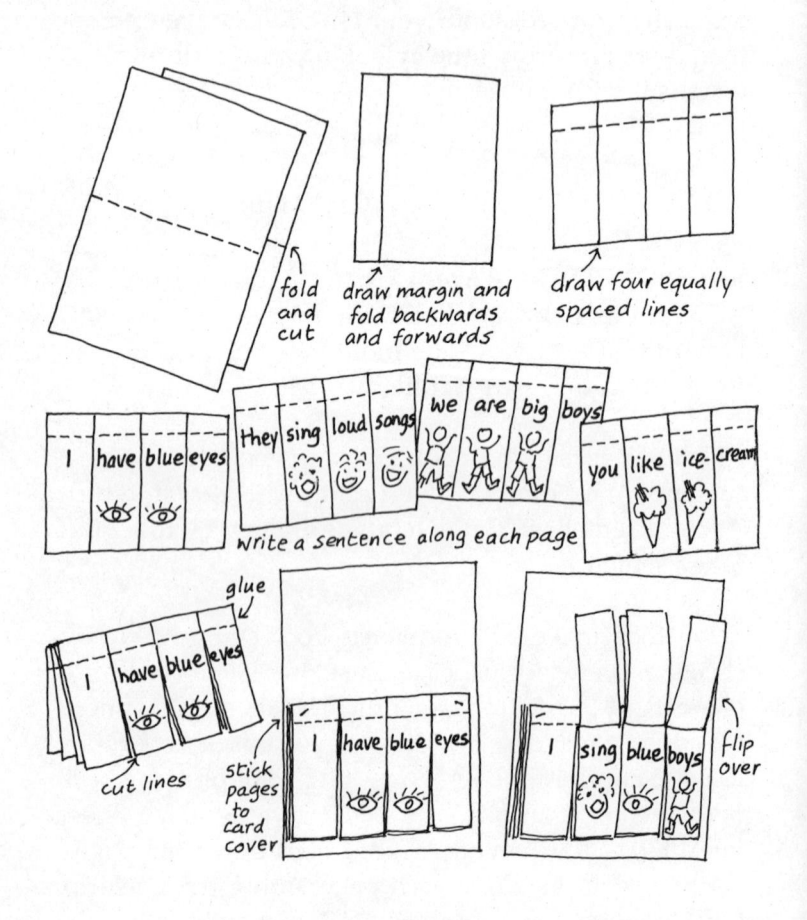

LEARNING THE RULES OF WRITING

* Help the children to make fun posters that will remind them of how to avoid continual errors. For example, if the word 'of' appears regularly instead of 'have', make a visual aid that can be posted on the wall somewhere. (Fig.2) Visual aids are meant to be memory joggers. Draw the children's attention to them at frequent intervals – they work like drips of water work on a stone.

Fig. 2

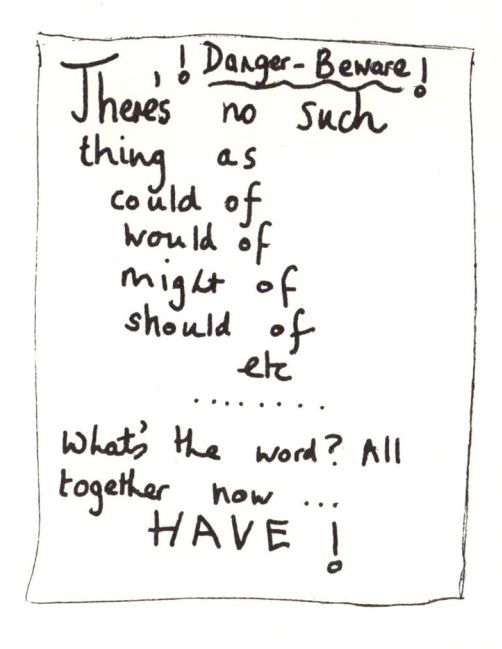

> Danger - Beware!
> There's no such thing as
> could of
> would of
> might of
> should of
> etc
> ....
> What's the word? All together now...
> HAVE!

* Together, make visual aid posters for all kinds of grammatical points. See Fig. 3 over the page.

Fig. 3

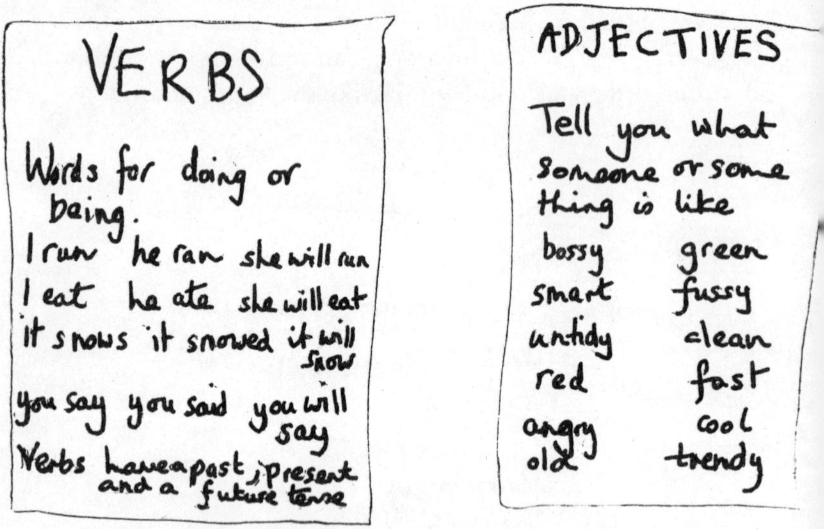

```
VERBS
Words for doing or being.
I run    he ran    she will run
I eat    he ate    she will eat
it snows it snowed it will snow
you say  you said  you will say
Verbs have a past, present
and a future tense
```

```
ADJECTIVES
Tell you what
someone or some
thing is like
bossy     green
smart     fussy
untidy    clean
red       fast
angry     cool
old       trendy
```

REINFORCING PUNCTUATION
* A tape recorder is helpful for learning punctuation. Get the children to tape themselves telling a story or anecdote. They then listen to the tape and write the words, putting in the punctuation they think they used with their voices. Listen to the tape again. Get someone else to read the written version, using the punctuation to show them how to read the piece. Check the two versions against each other.

Learning The Rules Of Writing

Look for the mistakes that keep occurring over and over again. Write passages together without those punctuation marks and help the children to read them aloud and put them in.

* To learn how speechmarks work, let the children read and write their own comic strips. They need to work out a short story, plan it in to a number of boxes (called 'frames'). Each frame has a picture of what's happening, a caption narrating the development of the story, and speech bubbles showing the characters talking. When the comic strip is finished get the children to write it again as a straightforward story, putting in direct speech instead of bubbles.

* Explain how contractions miss out a letter and use an apostrophe in its place. Use visual aids to show them, *'can't, won't, don't, let's, I'll, it's'* etc.

* Explain how ownership works for the apostrophe 's', and make a poster visual aid showing simple examples: *'John's coat, Sameer's computer, cat's tail'* etc. You need not go into the detail of how it changes for the plural (*boys' coats*) until they have really understood the concept.

* Make visual aids showing the various rules of punctuation. (See Fig 4 over the page.) You will need to go over the rules lots of times. Get the children to help you make the posters, making them applicable to them, so that they know exactly what they mean. The aids are to keep a reminder in front of them.

Fig. 4

> ## Speech marks
>
> Use speechmarks when someone speaks. *(I'm taking my dog for a walk)*
>
> Annie said, "I'm taking the dog for a walk."
>
> Don't use them when you're _reporting_ the speech.
>
> Annie said she was taking the dog for a walk.

REINFORCING SPELLING

* Make personal word dictionaries. You need to buy a small notebook with at least 26 pages. Get the children to write the alphabet in the book, one letter per page.

* Together, decide on words that they find they have particular trouble with. Write them in the relevant pages of the word dictionary.

* Equip the children with clear commercial dictionaries or a spelling dictionary, that work at their level, whatever that level is. Make sure they know how a dictionary is organised, it's not something you can take for granted. Begin by getting them to estimate which letter they think they might land on if they open the dictionary in the middle; in the first quarter; in the second quarter, etc. Which letter do they think will have the most pages of words? Which letter do they think might have the least? Help them to check whether they're right. Explain what the words shown at the top and bottom of the pages are there for. Help them to get used to using the dictionary by playing games. *'Find the L section.' 'Find the G section.' 'Who can be first to find the word. . .?'*, and so on. The more games you play, the more familiar they become with the dictionary and the less frightened they will be to use it as a tool for helping with their spelling.

* Make visual aid posters together, of the different spelling rules that they need to remember.

* Teach them how to use sound tricks and mnemonics to help them memorise words they frequently get stuck on. For example they might say 'frI-end' to remember the i and the e in 'friend', becAUse to remember the A and the U in 'because', BEAUtiful to remember the beginning of 'beautiful'. Build up ways of helping them to learn the kinds of words that trip them up, so that the moment they think of them, they remember their memory joggers.

* Teach them to study/write/see in order to learn new words. They should examine a new word carefully to note any bits that might trip them up. Next, they need to write the word in a flowing hand to get the feel of its movement. They now need to close their eyes and visualise the word (looking upwards, eyes closed, and to the left will help). Write the word, then check against the original. There is little point in copying new words over and over again because it means they are not taking the word as a whole but are breaking it up, doing part of it, looking again, doing the next part, and so on. Much better to tackle the word as a complete unit so that visual memory will enable them to see the whole thing.

REINFORCING HANDWRITING
* All of the letters need to be formed in the correct way right from the beginning. If children learn to print the words incorrectly, for instance forming an 'a' from the bottom up, when they come to do joined up handwriting the letters will be very difficult to join together and no flow will be achieved. The chart at the end of the book will show you the starting point for all letters.

* Children really enjoy doing handwriting patterns. They can make them as simple or as complex as they like, simply by colouring them in.

* A few patterns are shown (see Fig. 5). They get progressively harder as you go down the page. The idea is that all letters or shapes should be equally spaced and

Learning The Rules Of Writing

the risers and descenders should end at the same level. This is much trickier than it looks!

Fig. 5

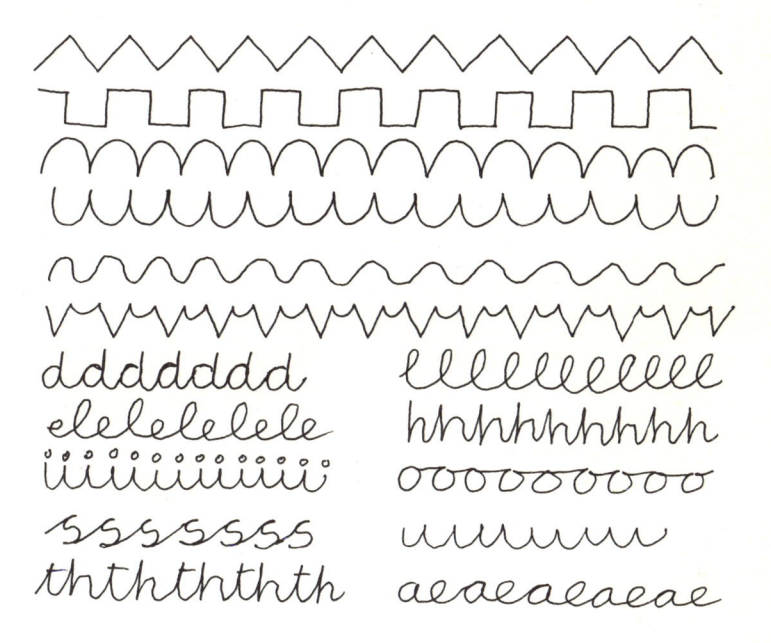

* The best way to start handwriting patterns is with a huge sheet of paper and fat wax crayons. The bigger the better. Encourage the children to get the feel of their hand and wrist flowing; it is this flow that makes for good handwriting. Gradually decrease the size of the paper and the tool so that the fine motor muscles are being more controlled – but the flow should never be lost.

* Doing writing patterns like this also helps to build up stamina for writing. Many children clutch their pencil so tightly that they experience real muscle fatigue after a very short time.

* You can do patterns like this around the edges of pages in margins, on letters and stories, or even, just one after the other, on 'samplers'. Make up your own patterns using all the letters of the alphabet and letter strings that are frequently found in words and turn the pages round so that you might have a line of letters the right way up then a line of letters the wrong way up. Look for the spaces between the lines, do the children always get exactly the same spaces? Let them decorate the spaces in between the letters with dots, stars, crosses, etc. Once they get going there'll be no end to their creativity!

* Stitch or staple sheets of card together to provide a good, solid booklet for writing patterns. Draw evenly spaced lines very finely in pencil so that they can be used to keep the lettering straight and then rubbed out.

* Encourage the children to 'publish' books of their favourite poems, culled from anthologies or written by themselves, in their very best handwriting. Decorate each page with handwriting patterns and embellish with finely drawn names and illustrations.

Don't insist on the pages being square-on to the children. Ideally they should slant slightly to the right for a right-handed writer and slightly to the left for a left-handed writer.

Chapter Six

WRITING IN SCHOOLS

In school, children are expected, from the beginning, to do many different kinds of writing.

DIFFERENT KINDS OF WRITING IN SCHOOLS

CREATIVE WRITING
Children are taught to do creative writing. This involves them making up:

* stories
* poems
* little plays
* captions for illustrations
* personal anecdotes

In these kinds of writing, the children are introduced to different forms of story and poem or rhyme, and use them as models for their own writing.

FACTUAL WRITING
They are also taught to do factual or informational writing. This involves them not only in writing about

* something they have done
* somewhere they have been
* something they have seen or learned about
* something they have heard or read about

but in getting the facts right as well!

METHODS OF TEACHING WRITING

WHOLE LANGUAGE APPROACH
In many classrooms you will find that reading and writing are taught hand in hand. Children will be encouraged to write freely in order to read.

In a classroom which uses a 'whole language' approach, you will see reading and writing activities going on all the time. For instance, even in the nursery, children playing in the 'Home Corner' will be encouraged to 'put out notes for the milk' or write down 'recipes' for baking. They will be persuaded to 'read books' to the teddies, to 'read and write' birthday cards, invitations, jot down notes on calendars, etc.

Quite often they are being engaged in these kinds of activities before they can read or write at all. The reason is that they are learning lots of skills that are important – for example, the fact that our writing in English goes from left to right and from top to bottom of the page. They will be learning which way the pages turn, what is the right way up, and so on.

In junior school a 'whole language' classroom will always be full of books and of children's writing. The children will be writing a huge variety of things – from short stories and poems to instructions on how to make a dodecahedron or how to play football or how to do macramé!

You will find the writing all over the classroom – no space will be too small for a piece of work or a child-made book to be displayed for public reading.

The children will be encouraged to keep different kinds of books to do their writing in – story books, poetry anthologies, serialised stories, topics, etc.

Spelling is taught alongside all the other reading and writing skills but the children are more likely to be expected to spell correctly in the writing that they do, than to be given formal 'spelling tests' once or twice a week.

Many schools use the idea of reading and writing partnerships, with the children pairing off with either children in their peer group or children older or younger than themselves. Often the partnerships work so well, with the children writing books for each other, that they spill over into the normal social roundabout of the school community and you find reading and writing partners, with two or three years' age difference, 'looking out' for each other in the playground!

This approach is a good one for building confidence and giving the children a real audience for their writing.

THE TRADITIONAL APPROACH

The more traditional teacher may treat reading and writing in a more formal way. They may use more comprehension exercise material, for example, where the child is reading the text first, reading questions, working out the answers, and writing them down.

In this classroom you may find work on the walls that has been drafted and 'fair copied' so that none of the processes of the writing are on view. Spelling tests may be a weekly feature of the teacher's strategies for teaching writing.

Of these two different methods of teaching English, one is very stimulating for the children, the other is much more traditional and perhaps easier for the teacher to monitor. Neither of them is 'right' or 'wrong'. They are simply different. In many schools these two kinds of teaching work quite happily alongside each other and you may find that your child experiences both techniques more than once during any phase of schooling.

The way the teachers teach can make a difference but it is best to remember that really – however they teach – they are all aiming at the same target. They want your child to become literate, and to reach their potential, as soon as possible.

Some children are happier with one approach and some with another. It is best, if your child is unhappy with the techniques used by the teacher, that you try to calm them down, reassure them that the teacher knows what she's doing, and try to make what you do at home dovetail with what's happening in the classroom.

The important thing is that your child's writing should be valued. The displays in classrooms will give you a clue about the way a teacher feels about writing. If the walls or frieze boards are covered with things that all the children have written (not just the 'best' ones), then you will know that the teacher values their writing. The children need to know that everything they write is appreciated, in order for them to be motivated to keep writing.

WRITING IN NURSERY/INFANT SCHOOL

First writing is usually factual. It may start with a five-year-old writing 'I saw a pondskater' after a pond-dipping trip. At this early stage the illustration will probably come first, because it acts as a form of planning for the writing.

Teachers are very aware that reading and writing and number are the most basic skills that children need to learn early. Some children will come into school already having a good grasp of the early stages of reading and writing. Others will arrive knowing nothing at all, sometimes barely able to talk.

The biggest problems for the early years teachers are children with very little language skill, because everything they can teach depends upon the children understanding the vocabulary, the reasoning, and having the ability to *think*. It is very difficult to think in a reasoning kind of way without language.

Towards the end of the infant school the teachers will expect the children to have learned most of the basics of writing. They will be expected to know that:
* writing is a means of communicating.
* writing is like speech in the way that it is for expressing ideas, feelings, beliefs.

* writing is a way of organising and developing ideas.
* writing can be a source of enjoyment.

The teacher will be working on specific skills, which will, again, weld the development of reading and writing together. The children will be learning to:

* write the letters of the alphabet.
* form the letters in the correct way.
* build up their knowledge of sound-symbol relationship.
* recognise and write letter patterns that occur over and over again in the spelling of words.
* build up a bank of words they can spell.
* remember prefixes and suffixes like 'un' 'ful' etc.
* use full stops, capital letters and question marks.
* use simple dictionaries.
* print, using capitals and lower case letters.
* write from left to right.
* keep their letters to a consistent size.
* space letters and words consistently.

Children will have had lots of experience of writing stories and poems and personal experiences. Much of their writing will have been 'one-off' pieces where the teacher discussed something with them and they sat down to write and draw about it. Many of these pieces will probably have been put together to make 'class books' or may have been used as classroom display.

Writing In Junior School

In junior school, lessons will probably become more formal. The kinds of writing children do will be broader and more varied.

Although they'll still be writing stories and factual texts, they'll also be trying to write reports or reviews of books or programmes they have seen, to write clear texts about subjects they have researched, to write drama scripts with dialogue and stage directions, to write clear instructions and explanations, to record science and maths investigations and to use some element of note-taking. They will be expected to:

* write for lots of different purposes.
* write for a much wider audience – other children, adults, the community, imagined audiences.
* use different kinds of writing for different products – for instance, they will be learning to write narrative, dialogue, explanation, instruction.
* write for much more demanding tasks, for example for pamphlets, advertisements, guidebooks.
* plan their work in an organised way.
* make notes – writing memory joggers rather than sentences.
* proofread – looking for their own errors in spelling, punctuation, grammar etc.
* use more sophisticated punctuation marks – for example, the exclamation mark, the comma, inverted commas, apostrophes.
* use more complex dictionaries.
* understand word roots and word families.

* distinguish between words that sound the same (homophones) but mean different things.
* search for synonyms.
* recognise silent letters in words.
* use contractions.
* use knowledge of language – for example, refer to an adjective, a verb, a vowel, a consonant.
* use cursive script (joined-up) handwriting.
* print clearly for diagrams and captions.
* use a neat script for finished work.

These guidelines are not, of course, definitive. We still, always, come back to the same premise, that not all children will reach the same stages at the same time.

There can be a huge difference between the most able and the least able child in any class – with possibly thirty different stages in between them!

Most children who have lots of support at home and become happy, natural, joyful writers, do not have problems at school with writing anyway, because they're so happy to do the tasks and activities, whatever they are, that they always achieve good results.

THE NATIONAL CURRICULUM

Before the National Curriculum, junior school children did a lot of 'topic' or 'project' work, which involved them in lots of research and huge quantities of writing. Unfortunately this writing mostly took the form of 'copying out of books' and didn't really help to develop writing skills at all. The difficulty was that, asked to regurgitate what they had learned from published books into their own exercise books the children had no way of reorganising the texts so that they made better sense. The children were reading from books which always gave the information in the best possible way – how could the children themselves improve upon it? So they ended up copying or, at the very most, paraphrasing.

The National Curriculum lays down very strict guidelines for what children should be taught, and when, in English.

WHAT CHILDREN ARE TAUGHT IN THE NATIONAL CURRICULUM

The aim of the English writing curriculum in schools is to get the children to write to a fairly structured programme, so that it actually becomes second nature to them to write in this way. Children are taught to:

1. *Plan*

This is the first stage of the writing. It includes talking about the content and the format of the writing. Children are taught how to plan for different kinds of writing – for creative writing, for informational writing, for formal writing. The plan might be quite different in each case but this stage will involve thinking time so that first ideas can be noted down and developed. As a general rule of thumb, the fuller the planning, the better the writing will be. Plans may be discussed or written down in note form.

2. Write The First Draft

This is where the plan is put into action, the writing accomplished in the time given – the ideas or message surrendered to paper, warts and all. The children are encouraged to think about message and not worry overly about the conventions.

3. Revise

At this stage the children are concentrating on content or message. They read through their work and decide whether and how they can possibly improve it. Have they missed out anything of importance? Can they move one sentence or paragraph to another place in the text, to make more impact or interest?

4. Proofread

Now they begin to look at the medium – the conventions. This is where they check the draft for any spelling errors they can spot, any punctuation errors, grammatical errors, omissions, repetitions, and so on. Word books, dictionaries, thesauri are all good, handy tools for them to have at this stage, so long as they are at the writer's level and easy for them to use.

5. Present A Good Copy

At this stage, medium and message converge. The children prepare a good, neat and correct copy from the draft. Illustrations, patterns and diagrams are all an essential part of this stage.

Even though the work doesn't go through quite such a formal structure, very early writers still follow, loosely, the same strategies. Even five-year-olds are encouraged to discuss their stories in order to plan them, write drafts, read those drafts aloud to make sure they say what they intended them to say, try to spot any errors and, sometimes, write them out neatly for publication.

DRAFTING

As we have seen above, children are taught to revise and proofread their work. This is called drafting and is now considered such an essential part of the writing process in schools, that it is worth going into in more detail.

Children work through the content of their writing themselves, looking for things that they want to change. These might be spellings, punctuation, vocabulary, or whole expressions of idea. It gives the writer the chance to 'discover' mistakes in the conventions of writing, and to rethink the way they have expressed what they want to say. It gives them the opportunity to go back and restructure or reorganise the product.

It's much healthier for children to realise from the start that what they have written is something that can be moulded and fashioned, rather than something that is fixed and totally unchangeable.

Of course, there isn't enough time for children to rewrite everything, but on the whole they are expected to redraft at least some of their work, in particular any creative items that they want to 'publish'.

The drafting process goes through several stages. Often the teacher will talk with the writer and help with ideas for those changes. If the writer is having problems, putting them into words aloud can usually help to pinpoint and clarify them in the writer's mind. The difficulty for the teacher is not to meddle or intrude upon the writer's intention by making suggestions that will perhaps take the writing in a direction that is not really the writer's choice.

SATS
Children's progress is tested by SATS (Standard Assessment Tasks) at 7, 11 and 14 which incorporate assessments of writing.

Key Stage 1
The Key Stage 1 test, at 7, is largely a reading test. The test is organised as a piece of comprehension material with questions. The children have to read the text and answer questions, in writing. They are marked on their ability to understand the text and write the answers clearly.

There is also a spelling test. This may take the form of a series of pictures with a space by each picture for the word to be written in. You can probably see the difficulties of this kind of spelling test. The first problem is that the child has to know what the picture actually represents. Suppose it is a bucket, or a mop – then the child has to know what those objects are called. The second huge problem, which cannot be overcome in this kind of test, is that the words can only ever be nouns. It is impossible to show a verb or an adjective, because how can they be illustrated in a fair way for a child?

Because of these difficulties the spelling test is

sometimes a piece of Cloze procedure. This is a piece of text where certain words have been left out. The child has to read the text, understand the word that is missing, and put it into the space. In some ways this is a fairer test, giving the opportunity to use different kinds of words, but it still has to assume that the child has a certain amount of language which is not *exactly* a writing skill.

Key Stage 2 and 3
The tests after 7 ask the children to do a piece, or more than one piece, of written work. These are marked according to content and use of punctuation, spelling and handwriting.

The children are usually asked to do a piece of imaginative work, i.e. a story, and a more factual piece. The topics are normally the kind of thing the children might have done many times in the classroom – 'Trip to the Moon', 'My School', 'My Best Friend' etc.

Usually the children are given space in which they should plan their work first and they are expected to show, in writing, that they can note down their ideas, develop them, prioritise them into a logical order, and then write them up as text.

How children approach these tests is crucial to how well, or badly, they do in them.

Some children see all tests as a challenge and an opportunity to show what they can do. They feel confident and positive from the moment they first look at the paper. Children who feel like this will always do their very best and achieve their potential. It's a self-perpetuating cycle. Their self-esteem will rise and the next test will see them even more confident.

Others do not find it so easy. It's as if a test of their knowledge and skills is a test of them as people and if they 'fail' the test then they know they will lose self esteem. If they are frightened and anxious, then their skills will largely desert them and they will work slowly and not finish, or they may work too quickly and make silly mistakes that they wouldn't otherwise make. They may not have time to go back and proofread and put their mistakes right.

PREPARING YOUR CHILD FOR TESTS

One of the ways you can help to prepare children for any writing tests, at any stage of their education, is by getting them to do timed writing.

Start with very short time periods of, say, five minutes and make it fun. *'How much can you write for me in five minutes, beginning now?'* They will invariably say, *'What shall I write about?'* so, to begin with, give them ideas.

As they get used to doing this kind of activity try saying, *'Write for ten minutes on the first thing that comes into your head!'* and so on. In fact, why not write together then swap writings?

You can have real fun, suggesting topics for each other, and even, later on, suggesting, *'Let's write something sad,' 'Let's write something happy'*.

You can build the time up to as long as the children seem willing to 'play' for, but don't let it become a chore. Fifteen to twenty minutes, two or three times a week, is probably the optimum amount.

It would be better not to go into proofreading mode – merely concentrate on the content. Later, when the children are so used to the exercise that they do it happily without any qualms, you can start to look at the spelling or the punctuation.

This kind of timed writing game will give them the confidence to be able to write on any topic that's suggested, during tests, without any anxiety. If it's something they do with you all the time at home why should they be afraid of it happening once in a while at school?

School Computers And Writing

All schools have computers these days and most schools have one in every classroom.

The children are encouraged, and expected, to use them to develop their writing skills in several different ways.

To begin with, there are programmes which are used for teaching spelling, punctuation, grammar. These are really not much different from the old question and answer books that children used to do for hours on end two or three decades ago. Their great disadvantage is the same as that of the books – often the learning doesn't transfer from the computer activity to the functional writing! It's easy to zap the right answer when you've only got to press a button and then whiz on to the next question. But do you remember to put those answers into practice when you're actually writing a story?

The other way the computer can be used, of course, is as a word processor.

This is a little more difficult in the classroom simply from the logistics point of view. With one computer and thirty-plus children, there's not a lot of time for anybody to 'have a go'. Often, two or three children work together round the VDU, trying to compose – though this sharing of the activity is not a bad thing at all, since ideas sometimes develop much better when they're shared.

But – there is always the problem of keyboarding. If the children have been polishing their keyboarding skills from the beginning then maybe they will actually get something done during their half-hour turn – if not then they'll be tapping out letters, one at a time, taking half an hour to produce a couple of sentences! And losing their composition direction at the same time!

Whether the spellcheck is an aid to developing the skills of spelling is a moot point! The writer can actually use a spell and a grammar/punctuation check if the programmes are available, but in many ways, although they make the work correct, they're not helping the children to improve their own learning, merely giving them a short cut to seeing their own, externally-corrected work in print.

A huge disadvantage is that while they are typing the children are not practising and developing their handwriting. But, of course, it is the ideal way to compose when the writer is focusing upon content and 'trying to get the words right' because they can go back and change things, move things about, use different words. In a way, it is the best way to show the children the flexibility of writing – it certainly doesn't ever have to be 'set in concrete' when they use a word processor.

The other advantage is that the work looks good when it's finished, particularly if the writer intends to 'publish' it.

Perhaps the ideal is for the children occasionally to use technology and often not! The difficulty there may be that once the children get 'hooked' into the computer, they may not want to go back to the hard work of writing by hand!

PRACTICAL ACTIVITIES

DRAFTING

To help the children with the redrafting process, let them keep several notebooks, which are their own personal possessions, not to be interfered with unless they ask you to look at them!

The first notebook needs to be exactly that. A notebook for notes. In this book the children can scribble down any ideas they have for anything they want to write. They may have ideas for stories, poems, factual accounts. Sometimes the ideas flow at the wrong time. But ideas get forgotten quickly so they need to be jotted down.

The format of this book should be completely informal. Encourage them to organise it in any way that works for them. One way of doing it is to jot down an idea (together with little illustrations, diagrams, whatever is necessary to jog the mind) and to draw a line straight across the page underneath it. This keeps it from being muddled up with the next idea. The first idea can be crossed off when it's been used or developed. Of course, sometimes several ideas work together. The way to deal with them is rewrite them in one block as one idea, then cross out the two or three that led to this development.

The second notebook should be a First Draft book. In this one, the children make their first drafts, getting down their ideas as quickly as they can, not worrying about handwriting, spelling, or any of the conventions. They are merely trying to trap the message before it disappears.

After writing the first draft they go back through it and make all their alterations on the text. If they want to have a go at a second draft, this is the book to do it in.

The third notebook should be for Presentation. This is where they draw their best margins, write their headings, do their underlining, use their best pen or pencil and really try to make the work look good. If they are going to present the work for publication, i.e. make a book of it, then they can miss out this stage if they want to.

If keeping notebooks doesn't really work for your children, try using a large lever-arch file full of plastic pockets. Each pocket can be for the continual stages of the process for one piece of writing, so that it would contain the original plan or notes, the drafts, and the final piece.

Save as much material as you can, because, apart

from anything else, children are fascinated to see the stages they went through at all times of their development to reach where they are now.

DISCUSSING WORK

First, make sure that your intervention is welcome and is not going to make the writer stop writing. Your aim is to help the development, not put them off.

Talk about the story or text. Encourage them to develop, expand and/or reorder the story if it needs it. To make some stories polished, taking bits out might be necessary. Show the children when something isn't necessary but accept the fact that they have a great deal of difficulty in deleting sentences they have written. It takes a lot of writing maturity to be able to 'abort'. During the discussion you should confirm all the skills the writers know and are using – say things like, *'You use a lot of letter sounds that are right in your words now,' 'You're learning to use lots more words,' 'You seem to be spelling very well now,' 'I see you use the dictionary whenever you need to, well done!' 'I like the way you use punctuation correctly'*.

At the end of the writing, encourage the children to re-read their stories aloud (often they will hear 'mistakes' that they do not see) and help them to evaluate by asking, *'Why did you choose to write this?' 'What do you really like about it?' 'Do you want to add anything?' 'Does your story say what you wanted it to say?' 'Shall we publish it?'*.

If the answer to the last question is *'Yes'* then discuss with them the form the publication will take, its format, what it will look like, how you are going to put it together etc. This is a problem-solving activity that will develop their thinking skills as well as aid their writing development.

Chapter Seven

SUMMARY

It cannot be over-emphasised that confidence and motivation are needed for children to reach their full writing potential.

On the whole, children start off feeling very confident. They think, from Day 1, that they can do anything they want to do. It's only when this self-confidence is knocked out of them that problems arise.

The pre-school child who presents you with a piece of scribble and tells you it's a story about the puppy who got off the lead and ran away, is certain that the picture or the words tell you exactly that. The infant child who writes that she saw a monkey at the zoo, even though it comes out as 'isumkyz' is just as happy that what she has written has communicated the story of the whole trip to the zoo to you. And, in a way, maybe she has, because what has come across in those few scribbled letters is her absolute joy at being able to write you a story about it. She will have a huge grin on her face when you and she read it together. And she needs no more motivation than the joy it gives her – and you.

As they begin to understand that there's a bit more to writing than just putting marks on paper, children's confidence can take a blow. Hopefully they rise to the challenge and assume that they can 'do it' too. Unfortunately many of them begin to think they can't and once they believe that they will fail, then fail they will. Unless you can catch them before they slip through the net!

KEEP YOUR CHILD MOTIVATED

THE NEED FOR A REASON TO WRITE
The first thing anyone needs, in order to write, is a reason to do so. There can be many good reasons for writing. The need to communicate by letter with someone. The need or inner urge to write something that you want to make public.

If the children never see you write anything it will be very difficult for you to motivate them into doing it for themselves, because they won't be able to see a reason for it. If you can live without it, why shouldn't they? The greatest reason you can give them for writing really is writing for the joy of it yourself.

In school, teachers are very aware that reasons for writing are crucial to the end product. However, it's quite difficult for them to give children 'real reasons' for writing. No matter how teachers wrap it up, the real reason for the writing children do day in and day out, is to practise and develop the children's writing skills. Good teachers know that they have to find and give the children better reasons for writing than that!

No matter what ideas the teacher gives for writing

about, the children will always try to work out for themselves:

* Why are we doing this?
* Who are we writing for?

Often, if you talk to the children after they've finished the writing, they'll feel happy about it only if it fits their idea of what they think the answers to those questions are. A lot of children never get past the idea that they're 'doing it for the teacher because it has to be done'. These are the children who usually find writing 'boring' or a 'waste of time'.

However, if your child is motivated to write at home, they are much more likely to be motivated to write at school.

AN AUDIENCE FOR WRITING
The 'Who are we writing for' is very important. If a teacher can offer the children an idea of an audience, someone to read their writing, then the motivation will be much stronger than if they think only the teacher is going to read it (and mark it!). Audiences can be anyone – the class, other children, other adults in the school, the community at large, examiners – it doesn't really matter *who* it is as long as the children know their labour is going to be rewarded by *someone reading their writing*.

However, it is much easier to provide an audience for your children at home. Of course, the children are always pleased when you show interest in their work and want to read it – unless they think you are just going to jump on the mistakes and criticise them.

It's even better if you can present that work to a wider audience. Family, friends, colleagues. If they know that what they are writing is going to be read by more people, then they will put in more effort to get it how they want it. They will be encouraged by praise of their efforts and the odd overheard remark that says they are, *'Good at spelling,' 'Have beautiful handwriting,' 'Write wonderful stories and poems'*. These kinds of remarks have a much better effect on their effort than negative ones that suggest they need to work harder on their spelling, tidy their work up, get some good ideas from somewhere.

How Writing At Home Instils Confidence

At home you have much the best opportunity to turn your child into a happy, confident writer, writing for the joy of it, than there can ever be at school. All the skills your child develops at home, will find their way into the school timetable and curriculum, and help them to blossom.

CHILDREN FEEL LESS ANXIOUS AT HOME
Children will feel none of the constraints or anxieties that they feel at school when asked to write. To begin with, they do not believe that you are the same as a teacher. Teachers are – in children's eyes – a different kind of person. Their expectations of the child are

totally different, and the child doesn't always know what those expectations are.

At home, it's different. You know each other so much better. You have a bond between you. The child knows, hopefully, you're not going to be disappointed in them, whatever your expectations are, rather that you'll be encouraging.

Also they have the confidence to ask you things they may not be able to ask the teacher – *'What do you mean exactly when you say. . . ?' 'Why do I have to write about x when I want to write about z?' 'What do you really want me to do?'*

Your relationship means that you're on a completely different footing, and it will show in the writing.

THE CHILD HAS A CHOICE OF SITUATIONS IN WHICH TO WORK

Be sensitive to your children's needs. Some writers are perfectly happy writing away at the kitchen table with the whole of family life going on around them. The blare of the radio, television or CD player may actually help them to concentrate. If this is how they want to work, it is probably the right way for them. Other writers need peace and quiet, they like to shut themselves away where no one else can bother them or get 'into their head' whilst they're trying to concentrate. If this is how they work best, try and help them to find a sanctuary.

At home you can talk through the product while it is being written or after it is completed. You have to learn to judge when your intervention is acceptable to the writer. Some children would rather concentrate their whole attention on getting from the beginning to the end of something and then looking through it. Others would rather have some feedback during the process of writing so that they know they are on the right lines. You need to be sensitive to the fact that children work in different ways. What suits one will not suit another. Try offering your comments and ideas during the writing stage and see how acceptable they are. If the writer gets cross and wants to be left alone then that is their way of writing. If they welcome your assistance then carry on, it will encourage them to keep going and to redraft.

CHILDREN ARE MORE CONFIDENT AT HOME

Because the writer feels so much more confident in writing for you, the writing will be more free, more experimental. It may have more 'voice'. 'Voice' is to do with 'ownership' of the writing. It's difficult to explain but, basically, if you are writing something that comes from some stimulus within you, writing for your own reasons, then you can be said to have true ownership of the writing – it all stems from you and is all an expression of you. That expression is 'the writer's voice'. Your 'voice' is different from anyone else's. It is what makes your writing recognisable as yours.

In school, the one thing that writing often lacks is 'Voice' because more often than not the topic has been suggested and organised by the teacher, it is not the writer's own choice. The writer feels little ownership of the work at all – it's been written really for the teacher rather than from an inner need to communicate a feeling, an idea, a fact.

CHILDREN FEEL LESS PRESSURISED AT HOME
The other fact is that, in school, writers are never writing alone. Usually thirty-odd children are scratching away at the same time – about the same topic! This means that there's an element of competition or a pressure to reach the 'right' standard, that is never present when you are writing together at home.

ABOVE ALL – BE ENTHUSIASTIC YOURSELF

One of the most important things children can absorb from you, is attitude. If you have a good and constructive attitude towards writing, then they will have too. Children copy their parents' behaviour, even without knowing it, and if you act as a good role model you can be sure they will assimilate your outlook.

Remember that learning to write usually involves making lots of mistakes, but that the making of those mistakes and the uncovering of them, is what leads to knowledge and to improvement.

Think about when your children were learning to talk – they experimented all the time. They began with single words, then added a second word, before shooting out little phrases. Finally they learned to speak in whole sentences. Writing is, in literacy, the equivalent of speaking. If you like, reading is the equal of listening – it is the receiving of communication – writing and speaking is the giving back of communication. Help the children to experiment with their writing in the same way that they experimented with their speaking.

Accept where they are and what stage they are at, even if you think they should be doing much better. Of course they *will* do much better, once you let them know that there is no blame attached to being at that stage, and that you can help them to make lots and lots of progress.

Because you can! You are in the prime position to make writing more than useful to them, more than learning, more than a chore. You are the person who can make their writing spontaneous, fun, a huge and satisfactory pleasure.

There is really nothing like the joy you will see on your children's faces when you read aloud and share with them the books they have made especially for you.

And there is nothing like the radiance they will feel inside from the confidence that you will inspire in them when you tell them how good, how brilliant, how absolutely lovely is their writing!

Appendix 1

Teach printing like this. Use lined paper, or draw lines, to help your child get the letter size right:

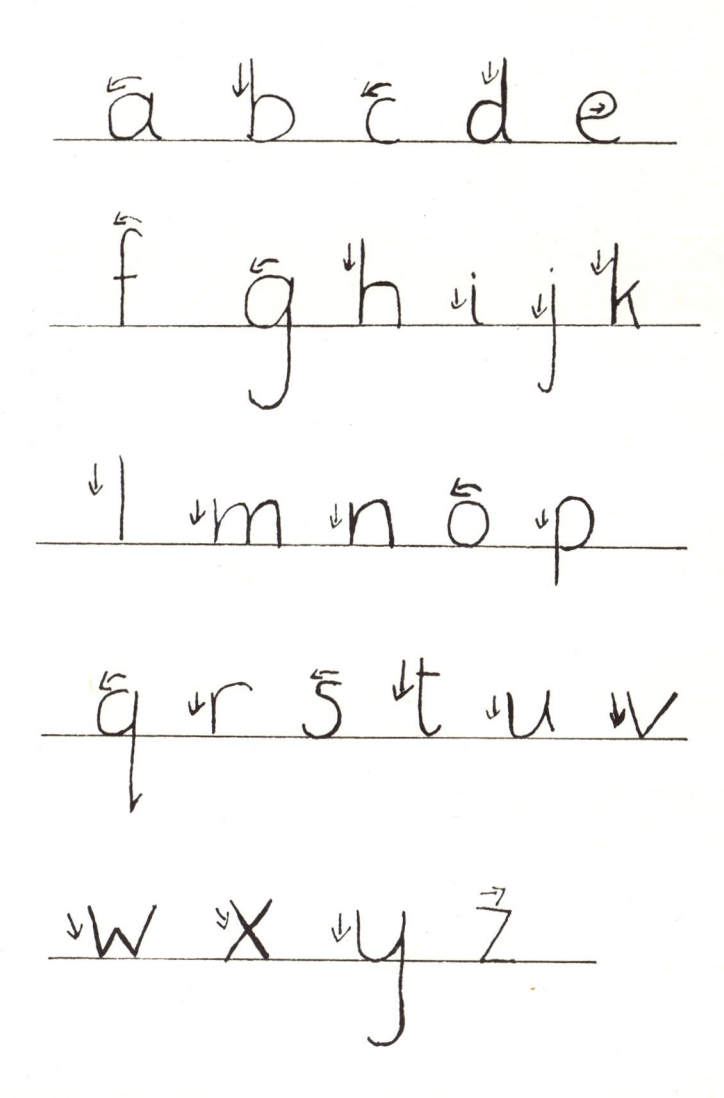

a b c d e

f g h i j k

l m n o p

q r s t u v

w x y z

WRITING SKILLS FOR PARENTS

For joined-up handwriting (cursive script) teach tails on letters, and practise letter strings, like this:

a b c d e f g h i
j k l m n o p q
r s t u v w x
y z

ar ar ar   th th th   es es es
im im im   ar ar ar   aw aw aw
chchchch   ing ing ing   ai ai ai
st st st   sh sh sh   oooooo
no no no   et et et   eth eth
str str str   ough ough ough

Some letters never join up – the 'b' and the 'p' for instance.

APPENDIX 2

THE NATIONAL CURRICULUM ATTAINMENT TARGET FOR WRITING:
Levels 1, 2 and 3 apply to Key Stage 1, for children aged five to seven years.

Level 1
Pupils' writing communicates meaning through simple words and phrases. In their reading or their writing, pupils begin to show awareness of how full stops are used. Letters are usually clearly shaped and correctly orientated.

Level 2
Pupils' writing communicates meaning in both narrative and non-narrative forms, using appropriate and interesting vocabulary, and showing some awareness of the reader. Ideas are developed in a sequence of sentences, sometimes demarcated by capital letters and full stops. Simple, monosyllabic words are usually spelt correctly, and where there are inaccuracies the alternative is phonetically plausible. In handwriting, letters are accurately formed and consistent in size.

They should understand how written English varies in terms of formality and discuss their choice of language.

Level 3
Pupils' writing is often organised, imaginative and clear. The main features of different forms of writing are used appropriately, beginning to be adapted to different readers. Sequences of sentences extend ideas logically and words are chosen for

variety and interest. The basic grammatical structure of sentences is usually correct. Spelling is usually accurate, including that of common, polysyllabic words. Punctuation to mark sentences – full stops, capital letters and question marks – is used accurately. Handwriting is joined and legible.

Levels 4, 5 and 6 apply to Key Stage 2, for children aged seven to eleven years.

* *Level 4*
Pupils' writing in a range of forms is lively and thoughtful. Ideas are often sustained and developed in interesting ways and organised appropriately for the purpose and the reader. Vocabulary choices are often adventurous and words are used for effect. Pupils are beginning to use grammatically complex sentences, extending meaning. Spelling, including that of polysyllabic words that conform to regular patterns, is generally accurate. Full stops, capital letters and question marks are used correctly, and pupils are beginning to use punctuation within the sentence. Handwriting style is fluent, joined and legible.

* *Level 5*
Pupils' writing is varied and interesting, conveying meaning clearly in a range of forms for different readers, using a more formal style where appropriate. Vocabulary choices are imaginative and words are used precisely. Simple and complex sentences are organised into paragraphs. Words with complex regular patterns are usually spelt correctly. A range of punctuation, including commas, apostrophes and inverted commas, is usually used accurately. Handwriting is

joined, clear and fluent and, where appropriate, is adapted to a range of tasks.

* Level 6
Pupils' writing often engages and sustains the reader's interest, showing some adaptation of style and register to different forms, including using an impersonal style where appropriate. Pupils use a range of sentence structures and varied vocabulary to create effects. Spelling is generally accurate, including that of irregular words. Handwriting is neat and legible. A range of punctuation is usually used correctly to clarify meaning, and ideas are organised into paragraphs.

Other books by the same author published by Piccadilly Press

READING FOR PARENTS
by Irene Yates

It's never too early or too late to help your child with reading!

Find out:
* How children learn to read and how reading ability is affect by different skills and practice

* Ways of making reading fun for your child through activities and games

* The benefits and faults of reading schemes

* How to recognise problems, help your child with specific difficulties and enlist the support of your child's teachers

'This practical guide has a sensible range of activities parents can adopt to make learning to read fun'
Times Educational Supplement

*Other books in the How To Help Your Child series
published by Piccadilly Press*

SPELLING FOR PARENTS
by Jo Phenix and Doreen Scott-Dunne

English spelling isn't as difficult or illogical as it seems once you understand it. Entertaining and easy to read, this practical guide for parents wanting to help their children to spell includes:

* and explanation of children's spelling development
* how to recognise children's strengths and weaknesses
* discussing children's progress effectively with teachers
* fascinating spelling trivia (did you know that William Caxton's 'u' didn't work very well, so he changed it to 'o' in words like done and wonder?)

'...offers refreshingly easy strategies for parents to use with children encountering difficulties with spelling...An optimistic book which would also be useful to adults with spelling problems'
The Independent

GRAMMAR FOR PARENTS
by Jerry George, with Clare Stuart

This is essential for any parent who wants to help their child with grammar. It includes: clear definitions of the terms we use to talk about grammar; explanations and examples of the major rules; suggestions for using grammar creatively to improve writing; and a list of the main grammar pitfalls.

'A short but packed with information practical guide to English grammar. An extremely useful book for parents.'
– School Librarian

MATHS FOR PARENTS
by Rosemary Russell

At last – a book for parents who want to help their children with maths but have shied away for fear of confusing them further!

Rosemary Russell discusses the different methods used in teaching maths in schools today. She explains how to build both your own and you child's confidence in maths; gives games you can play with your child to improve their maths without them even knowing; and what the National Curriculum means.

'...gives excellent support to parents defeated by modern teaching methods and National Curriculum demands.'
Times Educational Supplement

INFORMATION TECHNOLOGY FOR PARENTS
by Adrian and Rosemary Russell

Get a grip on the IT revolution...
Catch up with your children – and then you can help them!
Written by a teacher and an IT professional, this easy introduction to the world of Information Technology (IT) looks at:

* What IT is, and how much it matters
* How IT is being used in schools
* What the buzzwords mean
* The Internet
* The computer at home
* What the National Curriculum requires
* Ways in which you can help your child

'...Rosemary Russell has a refreshingly positive approach. Her explanations are clear...explains modern mathematical teaching methods, and perhaps more importantly, boosts parents' own confidence.'
Junior Bookshelf

ARE YOU EXPECTING TOO MUCH FROM YOUR CHILD
by Dr Fiona Subotsky

'...offers a fresh perspective for anyone having a hard time with their kids...uses case studies to show how parents of, say, a crying baby or a bolshy toddler are often worrying about behaviour that is, in fact, developmentally appropriate.'
Time Out

'...refreshing...rather than just dwelling on the behaviour of children, it invites them (parents) with the aid of short case studies, to reflect on their own attitudes and expectations.'
Times Educational Supplement

WELL DONE
by Ken Adams

Your child can't be brilliant at everything!
Most children have an area of weakness – verbal, mathematical or conceptual. Identify your child's weaknesses and help your child strengthen skills in these areas – without him or her even knowing!

'Adams is particularly good at explaining maths concepts and has lots of useful strategies to impart...good value.'
Time Out